RHODES

A full travel guide with 140 colour photographs
which will introduce you to the island 's history,
art andfolklore. It guides you round
archaeological sites, museums and others sights
of the island.

CONTENTS

PUBLISHED BY: DIMITRIS HAITALIS
EDITING & DTP: BARRAGE LTD
TEXTS: REGINA MOUSTERAKI
TEXT EDITING: MARIA MAVROMATAKI
ENGLISH TRANSLATION: COX and SOLMAN
ART EDITING: FOTINI SVARNA

PHOTOGRAPHS: HAITALIS PUBLISHING
CO. ARCHIVE

EDITIONS DIMITRIS HAITALIS
ASTROUS 13, 13121 ATHENS,
TEL.: 5766883

Introduction

p. 7 ▶

Mandraki: the entrance to the harbour is flanked by two bronze deer standing on columns and serving as a kind of emblem of Rhodes in modern times. In the background is the St Nicholas tower.

Rhodes, one of the Mediterranean's most beautiful islands, lies in the southernmost part of the Aegean Sea, very close to the shore of Asia Minor. The ancient Greeks were so taken with its charms that they associated its beneficent climate with a myth that has lived on down to our own times. According to this, Helios, the life-giving sun god, enchanted by the island's natural beauty, asked Zeus as a favour that he should be its protector and benefactor. Ever since then, Rhodes has been flooded with sunlight and the rays of its favourite god have showered their gifts upon it.

It would seem, though, that Rhodes has been favoured by all the gods, since throughout its history it has known moments of greatness and glory and emerged as one of the most important regions in the whole of Greece. The cultures which have developed on its soil have each enriched it with their own achievements and have left their mark upon it as one has succeeded the other. These marks have remained indelible down to the present, giving the impression that every part of the island is none other than a different plane in the mechanism of time. Next to

the white marble of the ancient temples and statues, the half-ruined walls of the settlements and sanctuaries where the gods of ancient Greece were worshipped, stand the little Byzantine churches with the gaze of the ecstatic figures in their wall-paintings fixed on the heavenly God of the Christians. A little further on, the narrow streets lead to medieval palaces and castles, from which you expect to see knights in armour charge forth. At the same time, from behind high walls the

domed roofs of Turkish mosques and the crossed arches of the low houses in the Turkish quarters make their presence felt.

Nevertheless, all these images from the past have not robbed Rhodes of the pleasures of modern life. On the contrary, they have made a crucial contribution to the island's development, making it one of the most cosmopolitan places in Europe. Thus the pace of its life has speeded up and it has become a tourist centre of

p. 8 - 9

Panorama of Mandraki with the St Nicholas tower and the picturesque windmills, dating from the time of the Knights. In the foreground is the New Market building.

the greatest importance. Its harbours are full of ships, yachts and fishing-boats, its beaches are covered with multi-coloured sun-shades and sun-tanned bodies, its hotels echo to the sound of every language under the sun, its streets are filled with tourist shops, restaurants, cafés, bars and discos, where music and dancing bring the night to life.

In fact, Rhodes can grant any wish of the holiday-maker. The island's capital and Faliraki can provide a good time that will be long remembered, the Old Town will enchant the romantic, the modern city will supply every need of the shopper, the indented coastline with its beaches will provide a cooling swim in the hot afternoons, and the parks, squares, and woods are ideal for quiet walks. At the same time, the mountain villages will give visitors some idea of local tradition and allow

p. 10

The Temple of Pythian Apollo, on the Ayios Stefanos hill or 'Monte Smith'.

them to breathe the scented air - and the aromas of tasty country cooking. At the local festivals, which are frequent, the visitor can enter into the rhythms of Greek music and dance. And those who want to learn about the history of Rhodes will find traces of it scattered everywhere, from the settlement of Cameiros, the cemeteries of Ialysos and the imposing rock of Lindos to the deserted monasteries, the churches of Filerimos, the forgotten castle of Monolithos, the palaces and fortifications of the capital, and the Turkish baths and mosques which bring the West closer to the East.

However, whatever are the visitor's wishes and expectations, no one can avoid feeling close by the shadow of the Colossus, the bronze giant of Rhodes, its protector the Sun, who will be there to halt the flow of time and link yesterday with today.

p. 11

View of the Old Town of Rhodes. The imposing Palace of the Grand Masters can be seen in the background.

Geography

The Greek archipelago, serving as a bridge to link East and West, a crossroads and a meeting-point for three continents - Europe, Asia, Africa - and three different worlds, was the birthplace of the most ancient civilisations. For centuries it attracted peoples to settle within its borders and was bustling with life at periods when mainland Greece was in decline.

In this world, at its south-eastern extremity, lies Rhodes, the fourth largest of the Greek islands. It has an area of 1,398 sq. kms, belongs to the Dodecanese group of islands, is 246 nautical miles from Piraeus, and, according to the 1981 census, has a permanent population of 90,963. Its shape is elliptical, and it has a maximum length of 77 km., while its greatest breadth is 37 km.

A 47 km. channel separates it from the island of Karpathos and a narrower one, of 37 kms, from the coast of Asia Minor. Rhodes, like the rest of the islands of the Aegean, was created by the fragmentation of Aegeïs, the continent which extended from the Ionian Sea to Asia Minor and the northern coast of what is now Crete. The island's terrain is mountainous.

Its rocks, which are of limestone and schist, form a mountain backbone in the centre of the island: Mt Atavyros with its peaks - Akramytis in the south-west, 823 m. at its highest point, Atavyros in the middle at 1,215m., and Profitis Ilias to the north (798 m.). The mountain mass gives place to plains which are of limited area, but fertile.

The island's coastline is indented with innumerable beaches, mostly sandy, wide bays, and headlands, such as Zonari in the north-east - on which the city of Rhodes stands - Lardos or Fokas in the east, Armenistis in the west, and Prassonisi in the south.

The latter is joined to the rest of the island by a narrow spit of land and becomes an islet when the sea level rises. Rhodes has a Mediterranean climate, with an average temperature of 18 - 200, mild winters, and cool summers (thanks to the cooling north-easterly which blows in the summer months). It has a high number of hours of sunshine (some 300 days a year) and high humidity.

It is the sunshine and humidity which account for the island's lush vegetation. Rhodes, though mountainous, is green all over, the only exception being the area around Mt Atavyros, which underwent deforestation

p. 14

The little harbour of St Paul at Lindos is one of the prettiest places on the whole of Rhodes.

during the period of Turkish rule as a result of uncontrolled woodcutting.

Typical of its flora are conifers, plane trees, oaks, thyme, capers, cyclamens and many other kinds of wild flowers. Of its fauna, a kind of deer, the platóni, which lived in the woods from prehistoric times, is particularly associated with the island.

The economy of Rhodes, before the tourist boom, was based on farming and stockbreeding (chiefly cattle, but with some sheep and goats). Nowadays, large numbers of the islanders are employed in some way in the tourist industry, while the rest continue in the traditional occupations. The island's principal products are olive oil, wine, vegetables and citrus fruit.

The capital is the city of Rhodes, which is also its port and the starting-point for a good road network which takes in its villages and places of interest.

p. 15

The coastline of Rhodes forms itself into countless beaches and indented coves.

16

The Traditions of Myth

The attraction which Rhodes has for visitors is not due only to its natural beauty and its individual character, but also to the very important role which it has played in the history of Greece. While we have the testimony of archaeological research and the written sources, an outline of the remote past of the island can be disentangled from a series of myths which have been preserved down the centuries.

Rhodos (Rhodes), as we are told in one of Pindar's Odes, was the daughter of Poseidon and Amphitrite (or, according to another version, Aphrodite) and the beloved of Helios, the sun god. When, one day, the gods were sharing out the earth among themselves, Helios, faithful to his duties, was away, making his daily journey round it, and so was not included in the share-out. When he returned, Zeus, not wishing to be unjust to him, prepared to repeat the process. But in the meantime Helios had seen an island of great beauty jutting from the depths of the sea. This he requested should be his portion and this he chose as a suitable spot for his union with the nymph Rhodos. Six sons, termed Heliades, were born to the couple, together with one daughter, Electrione, who died a virgin. Helios's first-born son, Cercaphos, himself had three sons, Lindos, Cameiros, and Ialysos. These three divided their father's land between them and each founded a city which bore his name.

Another myth about the name of Rhodes and its earliest inhabitants relates that it was first settled by the Telchines, sons of Pontus and Thalassa. The Telchines were very skilled in the crafts of fire and metals - and in magic. Posei-

p. 17 ►

Marble head of a statue of the Hellenistic period (late third - early second century BC) depicting the god Helios. In the hair, the holes to hold the metal rays which would have crowned the deity can be seen. (Rhodes Archaeological Museum - Great Aphrodite Room).

don fell in love with the sister of the Telchines, Halia, by whom he had six sons and a daughter, Rhodos, who gave her name to the island. One day, Aphrodite asked permission from the Telchines to put in at the island and was refused. In order to be revenged, the goddess put a curse on them that they should commit incest with their mother and that the whole island should be covered with water. The Telchines were warned of this by Zeus and fled in good time, leaving their sister behind. For a long time, the plains of Rhodes were covered with water. When, however, the god Helios fell in love with Rhodos, he bathed her in his rays and thus their warmth evaporated the water which covered the land.

Another myth, clearly connected with the arrival of the Minoans on Rhodes, has as its hero Althaemenes, grandson of Minos. Althaemenes, wishing to foil an oracle which had foretold that he would kill his father, Catreus, left Crete and settled on Rhodes, where he founded a settlement to which he gave the name of Cretenia, a reference to his homeland. On the summit of Atavyros he build a temple to Zeus. After many years, Catreus arrived on the island in search of his only son, but Althaemenes did not recognise his father at a distance, and, thinking that he was a pirate, killed him, thus fulfilling the oracle. When he learnt the tragic truth, he asked that the earth would open up and swallow him, and his wish was fulfilled. Althaemenes, a tragic figure in some ways reminiscent of Oedipus, was honoured as a hero by the Rhodians. Another hero of myth, Tlepolemos, is associated with the settling of the Dorians on Rhodes. He came from Tiryns, on mainland Greece, and was the son of Heracles and Astioche. He left his home and settled on Rhodes after murdering his father's uncle.

Tlepolemos was killed at Troy by the leader of the Lycians and ally of the Trojans Sarpedon. In his honour, the Rhodians held a festival called the 'Tlepolemia'.

Helen of Troy was also worshipped in a sanctuary on Rhodes, under the epithet of Dendritis. Yet another myth is

p. 18

Mosaic of the Hellenistic period showing an actor's mask.

associated with this cult: Helen, after the Trojan War, arrived, pursued, on Rhodes, which was then ruled by the widow of Tlepolemos, Polyxo. As soon as Polyxo heard of this, she planned to avenge the death of her husband, and ordered her soldiers to capture Helen and hang her from a tree (déndron), hence the name Dendritis. Besides Althaemenes and Tlepolemos, another hero of Rhodes was Phorbas. Tradition tells us that Rhodes was once overrun with snakes (Ancient Greek óphis) and was called Ophiousa. In despair, its inhabitants sought the help of the Delphic Oracle. The Pythia replied that Phorbas, a member of the Thessalian tribe of the

Lapithae, alone could solve the problem. The Rhodians sought out Phorbas, invited him to come and live with them, and ever afterwards honoured him as their saviour.

Myth also relates that Rhodes was visited by Danaos, with his daughters the Danaids, and that Danaos built a temple at Lindos for the worship of Athena. Another visitor to the island was Cadmus, king of Phoenicia, who was looking for his sister Europa. During his stay, he built a temple to Poseidon and dedicated a bronze cauldron with an inscription in Phoenician script to Athena. This is mythology's way of explaining the introduction of the Phoenician alphabet.

pp. 20 - 21

Among the divinities worshipped on Rhodes, Apollo occupied a special place. The Rhodians built a temple to him on the acropolis hill of Ayios Stefanos or 'Monte Smith'. The photograph shows the restored Temple of Pythian Apollo.

History of the Island

PREHISTORIC PERIOD

p. 22

Part of a female statue in marble, a fine example of the art of Rhodes in the Hellenistic period. (Rhodes Archaeological Museum).

According to the historical sources, the island's first inhabitants must have arrived on Rhodes, as on most of the islands of the Aegean, before 3000 BC, that is, in the Neolithic period. Sporadic finds (sherds and stone vessels) in a cave on Mt Koumelos and at Kalythies support this conclusion. Furthermore, certain place-names, such as Atavyrion or Atavyris, Cameiros, Lindos, and Ialysos, indicate the presence of pre-Greek tribes.

Around 1550 BC, at a time when the Minoans ruled the Aegean, Cretans settled on Rhodes and set up a trading station on its north-western coast, near what is now the village of Trianta.

When the Minoan civilisation began to decline, the place of the Minoans as rulers of the Aegean was taken by the Mycenaeans, who, while absorbing many features of Minoan culture, set up trading posts in Sicily, Crete, Cyprus, Asia Minor and the islands of the Aegean in the course of their expansion. One of the islands on which they settled was Rhodes (1450 BC), where they first of all founded Ialysos, merging it with the Minoan settlement near Trianta. Other small settlements subsequently grew up and in a short while the Achaeans, an alternative name for the Myceaeans, had overrun the island.

This was a period of great prosperity for Rhodes. Some indication of this is the statement of the poet Pindar that because Zeus greatly loved the Rhodians, he showered them with golden rain. Information about the Mycenaean period on Rhodes has been derived from investigations of the prehistoric cemeteries of Ialysos (at Moskou Vounara and Makria Vounara in the foothills of Filerimos) and of Cameiros (at the village of Kalavarda).

CLASSICAL PERIOD

The Achaeans were succeeded in 1100 BC by the Dorians, who, starting out from the Argos region, established themselves on Rhodes - in areas which had already been flourishing in the Mycenaean period. The Dorian settlers of the south-eastern Aegean were originally divided up into six autonomous states, of which two were on the coast of Caria with their headquarters at Cnidus and Halicarnassus, one on Cos, and the remaining three on Rhodes.

Thus Rhodes was divided up into three regions: Cameiris in the west, and Lindia and Ialysia in the southern and northern halves of the island, respectively. These areas constituted three independent city-states: Cameiros, Lindos, and Ialysos. In 700 BC, the six Dorian states formed themselves into an amphictyony (a political and religious federation), known as the Dorian Hexapolis, with the sanctuary of Triopian Apollo, in the region of Cnidus (at what is today Kavo Krios, opposite the city of Cos), as its centre. After their unification, the three city-states of Rhodes lived peaceably as a federation, since they realised that, isolated as they were from the rest of the Greek world, it was only if they were united among themselves that they could survive and acquire strength.

In the eighth century BC, the Rhodians transcended the closed economy of their island by developing trade

◀ p. 23

Lindos was one of the three areas of Rhodes where the Dorian colonists chose to settle. The acropolis of Lindos is dominated today by the relics of the Temple of Athena Lindia.

with areas in Asia Minor (Miletus) and Crete, and by
founding colonies at the cities of Tarsus (800.BC) and
Al Mina (725 BC) on the Asiatic shore. In the second
half of the eighth century, they adopted the Phoenician
alphabet. However, although they shared their fates as
a federation, each of the city-states followed its own individual course.

Thus, Cameiros and Ialysos, in the fertile western part
of the island, based their economy on farming, while
Lindos, in the east, with less fertile land but a strategic
position for controlling shipping to the East, developed
a maritime character. It acquired a strong fleet, and between the eighth and sixth century, developed into a
naval power and a commercial centre. It began to decline in the early fifth century BC, when the Persians
made their appearance in the Aegean. In the seventh
century BC, the Rhodians developed commercial relations with Cyprus, with ports in the eastern Mediterranean, with Corinth, Samos, and the Cyclades. In 688
BC, they established the colony of Phase-
le on the coast of Pamphylia, with a
view to servicing the Rhodian vessels which plied along the Asia Minor coastline.

p. 25

*Beaked vessel of the
Mycenaean period
from Ialysos (Rhodes
Archaeological
Museum - 1st
Pottery Room).*

At the time of the founding of
Phasele, the Rhodians, together
with the Cretans, also colonised
Gela in Sicily, while at the end
of the seventh century BC,
they founded colonies on the
Balearic Islands and in Spain.

During the sixth century BC,
Cameiros and Ialysos had an
aristocratic form of gov-
ernment, while at Lin-
dos, Cleoboulos, one of
the 'Seven Sages' of antiq-

uity, established a tyranny. During the same century, Cameiros and Lindos minted their own coins. Those of Cameiros show a fig leaf and those of Lindos the head of a lion.

p. 26

Grave stele of the Hellenistic period, showing a dead warrior. (Rhodes Archaeological Museum - Timarista Room).

Ialysos minted coins in the fifth century with the head of an eagle as its emblem.

It was not only trade, but also the arts which flourished at this period. Rhodian pottery alone could compete in quality with that of Corinth.

In addition, an important goldsmiths' workshop developed on the island in the seventh century; this, in spite of Cretan and Eastern influences, managed to shape its own individual style.

In 491/90 BC, the Persian general Datis besieged Lindos. The inhabitants put up a brave resistance, in spite of a shortage of water. In the end, Datis abandoned the siege and went away.

During the Persians' second campaign, Rhodes was conquered and joined the Persian side, contributing 40 ships at the Battle of Salamis in 480 BC.

After the Persian Wars, Lindos lost its influence and Ialysos came to the forefront. As a city with an agricultural economy, it had suffered less from Persian expansionism. During the period after the Persian Wars, it was ruled by the aristocratic family of the Eratides, one of whose members, Diagoras, won a victory in the Olympic Games of 464 BC which made Rhodes famous throughout the Greek world. When the

first Athenian Alliance was set up in 478/77 BC, the three cities of Rhodes joined it and paid the tribute required of them. Thus, during the Peloponnesian War, the Rhodians, as members of the League, fought on the side of the Athenians. In 412.BC, following the defeat of the Athenians in Sicily, the son of Diagoras, Dorieus, who had fled to Thurii in Lower Italy after being condemned to death by the Athenians, returned to his native island and persuaded his fellow-countrymen to desert the Athenian League and join Sparta. One year later the Rhodians, following negotiations, decided on the unification of their three cities.

They drew up a 'charter', according to which Cameiros, Ialysos and Lindos would form a new city under a single administration, with a popular assembly, a boule ('parliament') and three prytaneis (chief magistrates). The division of the population into three 'demes' was retained, but now their sole responsibility was the settling of local issues.

The new city overshadowed the prestige of the old. It was founded in the north-eastern extremity of the island and was built on the Hippodamian town-planning system. Its official name was 'the Deme of the Rhodians' and its protecting deity was the sun god Helios, whose priest was archon (presiding magistrate) each year.

In 396 BC, the Rhodians, taking the opportunity of the Spartans' conflict with the Persians, decided to defect from the Spartan camp and during the course of the

Asia Minor campaign were on the side of the Persians. The city of Rhodes developed into a meeting-place for emissaries of those Greek cities with anti-Spartan tendencies and the envoys of the Persian satraps who were in charge of carrying on the war against the Spartans. In the same year, Dorieus visited the Peloponnese to try to bring about an uprising against the Spartans, but was soon arrested and put to death.

In 364 BC, when the Boeotian fleet came out into the Aegean under Epaminondas, Rhodes was for a short period its ally. In 357, with the encouragement of Mausolus, satrap of Caria, Rhodes concluded an alliance with Byzantium, which was following a policy hostile to the Athenians. Together with the Rhodians, the inhabitants of Chios, Cos and other cities also defected. The war which followed, between the Athenians and their apostate former allies, ended in the defeat of the Athenians at Embata in 355 BC.

This was the period in which Mausolus extended his rule beyond the borders of Caria, indirectly wielding power in Rhodes as well.

In 351, his successor, Artemisias, besieged the city and destroyed the island's fleet. The Rhodians sought the help of the Athenians in vain, and it was only after the death of Artemisias that they managed, in 340 BC, to drive out the Carians for good.

With emergence of the Macedonians to the forefront of political and military affairs in 332, the Rhodians allied themselves to Alexander the Great. They agreed to the installation of a Macedonian garrison in their city and gave their assistance to the Macedonians in the siege of Tyre. After the death of Alexander, they drove out the Macedonian garrison and established relations with the Ptolemies of Egypt. Alexander's other successor, Antigonus, sought their help in the war he was waging against the Ptolemies. Their refusal to involve themselves in this conflict led the son of Antigonus,

p. 27

The stele of Crito and Timarista, one of the most characteristic works of the fifth century BC.

p. 28

Marble statuette of Bacchus from Cameiros, dating from the Hellenistic period. (Rhodes Archaeological Museum - Room of the Lesser Aphrodite).

Demetrius, to attack Rhodes in 305 BC. His siege of the city lasted a year. The numbers of Demetrius's forces were unprecedented for the period: 40,000 soldiers and 30,000 men skilled in siege operations equipped with the latest 'technology' in siege engines of the time. Rhodes, however, thanks to its strong walls, was able to resist successfully and Demetrius withdrew, leaving behind him most of his siege equipment. This the Rhodians sold and built with the money a statue dedicated to their patron Helios - the famous 'Colossus of Rhodes'. Through the mediation of Antigonus and Ptolemy a treaty was signed safeguarding the Rhodians' independence.

The 150 years which followed were for Rhodes a period of great economic prosperity. The island became a centre for entrepot trade, a staging-point for all the vessels coming from mainland Greece, the Euxine Sea, Phoenicia, and Palestine. The ships of the Rhodians' own strong fleet carried their goods to every part of the Mediterranean, as far as Carthage in the west and Mesopotamia in the east.

In the third century, almost all the trade in the region was in their hands. At this time, the island was adorned with no fewer than 3,000 statues, and the population reached 300,000. In the post-war period around 220 BC, the Rhodians were able to prevent the city of Byzantine from imposing a tax on cereals passing through the Hellespont.

Rhodes suffered a major earthquake in 227 BC which destroyed part of the city and its fortifications and demolished the Colossus. Almost all the Greek cities sent financial aid, which the Rhodians used to rebuild their city, but they did not re-erect the Colossus, invoking an oracle to the effect that to do so would be a cause of disaster for the island.

In the late third century BC, another Macedonian, King Philip V, took the centre of the political stage. The

Rhodians, threatened by his expansionist policies in the Aegean, formed an alliance with Byzantium, Pergamum, Cos, and Rome. In 197 BC, they successfully resisted Philip at Cynoscephalae, while in 190, they took part in the sea battle of Side, led by Eudamus, against Hannibal, then the leader of the naval forces of Antiochus the Great, King of Syria, and the Romans' enemy. The Romans rewarded them for the part which they played in this war by ceding to them part of Caria and Lycia. Rhodes continued to be all-powerful. It formed alliances with cities of Asia Minor and took under its protection 'the commonwealth of the islanders', which had as its centre the sacred island of Delos.

ROMAN PERIOD

In the meantime, Philip V had been succeeded on the throne of Macedonia by Perseus, the last king of the Macedonians before their submission to the Romans. The Rhodians maintained friendly relations with Perseus and refused to help the Romans in a war which they were waging against him. After the defeat of Perseus at Pydna in 167 BC, the Romans punished Rhodes by recognising the independence of Lycia and a part of Caria, and in 166, in order to damage its trade, they declared the port of Delos free of taxes. This was a major blow to the economy of Rhodes. Its revenue from taxes imposed on merchandise on vessels in transit had formerly amounted to 1,000,000 drachmas, while after this measure of the Romans it fell to 150,000 drachmas.

In 164 BC, the Rhodians entered into an alliance with the Romans which imposed on them the obligation of taking part in their military operations. Thus they took part in the Third Carthaginian War and in the campaigns against Mithridates, King of Pontus, although they had previously maintained friendly relations with him. During the period of civil war at Rome, Rhodes was forced to side with one or other of the rival camps. Thus, when in 44 BC Cassius and Brutus sought their aid against their enemies in Asia Minor, the Rhodians replied that they would first have to have a decision from the Senate.

This stance angered Cassius, who captured the city after a siege, took over part of the fleet and destroyed the rest, put to death large numbers of citizens, chiefly philosophers and artists, and stole and carried off to Rome the island's treasures and works of art. After this, Rhodes sank into obscurity and in 155 AD was again struck by a catastrophic earthquake.

BYZANTINE PERIOD

In the meantime, Christianity had made its first appearance on the island, following the visit of St Paul in 57 AD, and Rhodes was represented at the First General Council of the Church (325 AD) by Bishop Euphronius. After the division of the Roman Empire into its eastern and western parts, the island was incorporated, in political terms, into the Eastern Roman State and became, from the time of Diocletian (297 AD) to the end of the sixth century, the capital of the Eparchy of the Islands.

During this time, its walls were rebuilt and it enjoyed a relatively short period of peace.

In 515 AD, yet another earthquake laid the city of Rhodes in ruins. This was followed by a difficult time for the island. In 620 AD, it was conquered by the Persians under Chosroes and, after the defeat of the latter, by the Byzantine Emperor Heraclius. In 653, it was taken by the Moabite Arabs, who gathered together the fragments of the Colossus and sold them to a Jewish merchant. In 717/18, it fell into the hands of the Sara-

p. 33

Relief tombstone of Petrus de la Pymorage (1402). It shows a knight in full armour in an attitude of prayer. According to the inscription which runs round the tombstone, Petrus de la Pymorage was governor of Rennes in Brittany. The coat-of-arms of the knight's order can be seen in the upper part.

cens and was looted in 807 by the Seljuk Turks of Harun al-Rashid, Caliph of Baghdad.

It was in 1082 that the Venetians, having obtained permission from the Byzantine Emperor, established a trading station on the island.

In 1191, Philip II of France and Richard the Lionheart stopped off at Rhodes on their way to the Holy Land to take on board supplies and to recruit mercenaries.

The Rhodian fleet took part in the Crusades, but when, in 1204, Constantinople (Byzantium) fell to the Franks of the Fourth Crusade, the Governor of the island, Leon Gavalas, unopposed by the Franks, proclaimed himself ruler ('Caesar') of Rhodes and minted his own coinage. In 1224, the Emperor of Nicaea, Ioannes Doukas Batatzes, took the island and forced its ruler to do homage to him. Gavalas was succeeded in 1240 by his brother Ioannes, who collaborated with the Emperor of Nicaea against the Latins. In 1248, the Genoese took the island.

When Constantinople was recovered by the Byzantines in 1261, the Emperor Michael Palaeologus, wishing to maintain good relations with the Genoese, ceded them sovereign rights

over territories of the Byzantine Empire, among which was Rhodes (1278). The city walls were repaired by the Byzantines in 1275.

THE RULE OF THE KNIGHTS

In 1306, the Genoese admiral Vinioli sold Rhodes, together with Cos and Leros, to the Order of the Knights of St John of Jerusalem.

p. 34

The city walls with the Sea Gate, which is flanked by two imposing towers. Between them, over the gate, St John, the Blessed Virgin, and St Peter are shown in relief, together with the coat-of-arms of D'Aubusson (1478).

The people of the island and the Byzantine garrison put up a strong resistance to the Knights for three years, but in the end they succumbed and thus, on 15 May 1309, Rhodes effectively came under the rule of the Knights of St John.

The Order of the Knights

The Order of the Knights makes its first appearance in history in the early twelfth century, when Pierre Gerard or

Gerard Tenque, a figure even today surrounded by mystery, arrived in Jerusalem.

It would seem that he was the founder of the Order, which took its name from his patron saint, St John. To begin with, the Order was of a religious and philanthropic nature, but after Gerard's death, his successor, Raymond du Pays, the first to bear the title of Master, invested it with a military character.

In the twelfth century, the Knights of St John played an important role in the struggle against the Muslims in the Holy Land. Having acquired a vast fortune from donations and with the support of feudal Europe, they managed to hold on to their bastions in Syria and Palestine until 1247, when Jerusalem fell into the hands of the Arabs.

In 1291, the Knights were forced to leave the Holy Land and took refuge in Cyprus, where they remained until 1306. In 1309, they installed themselves in the city

p. 35

The Koskinou or St John Gate.

of Rhodes and from then on acquired the name of 'Knights of Rhodes'.

The members of the Order were drawn from the Catholic countries of Europe and were divided into seven national groups or 'Tongues': those of Provence, Auvergne, France, Italy, Aragon (which included all those members who came from the Iberian peninsula), England, and Germany. Later, the Tongue of Aragon was sub-divided into those of Aragon and Castille. Each Tongue had its own coat-of-arms and leader, who belonged to the order of knights.

The members of the Order were divided into three classes, depending upon their descent: knights, who held all the major military and administrative offices, chaplains, from whom the clergy of the Order were drawn, and serving brothers, whose task was the care of the sick.

The knights were always drawn from noble families,

p. 36

The Gate of St Paul, near the tower of the same name and the Naillac Tower.

whereas the chaplains and serving brothers, though not nobles, were from the families of freemen and never serfs. The administration of the Order and of the state was in the hands of the Grand Master, who always came from the class of the knights and, consequently, was of noble birth. He held office for life and was elected by the members of the Order.

He was assisted by a council - the 'Chapter' - which was made up of the Bailiffs (leaders) of the Tongues. Each of these was charged with specific duties within the state machine.

From 1309 to 1522, the period of the rule of the Knights of St John over Rhodes and the other islands of the Dode-canese (with the exception of Karpathos, Kasos, and Astyp-alaia), 19 knights, starting with De Villaret and ending with Villiers de l'Isle Adam, held office as Grand Master. Of these, 14 were of French descent.

The official language for the documents of the Order and of the state was Latin, while the members of the Tongues communicated with one another in French. The spiritual ruler of Rhodes was the Pope. The Order ap-pointed a Latin archbishop, on whom the Greek - as they termed him - metropolitan was dependent. The Rhodians they called 'Colossians', after the Colossus.

During the rule of the Knights, Rhodes, even though under foreign sovereignty, managed to emerge from ob-scurity and to enter on a new period of prosperity. Trade and maritime contacts with East and West developed to a significant degree, while major commercial and bank-ing companies from Italy, France and Spain established themselves on the island.

This state of affairs favoured brisk building activity, in which the influences of the West are apparent. Fine ex-amples of the architecture of the time have survived un-til the present day (see: A Tour of the City of Rhodes).

THE RULE OF THE TURKS - MODERN TIMES

In 1480, Rhodes was unsuccessfully besieged by Sultan Mohamet II. On 28 July 1522, Suleyman II the Magnificent resumed the siege with a force of 100,000 men. The Knights and the people of the island put up a firm resistance. Damage done to the walls by the attackers was repaired by the besieged. Perhaps the island would have survived the siege had not a disaffected knight, D'Amaral, showed the Turks the weakest point of the castle. The traitor and two accomplices were put to death, but the Turks captured the city.

Following an agreement with Suleyman, the Knights left Rhodes with all their possessions, unlike the islanders, who were left behind to endure every kind of suffering.

A great massacre of the inhabitants followed the Turks' entry into the city, which, according to tradition, stopped only when the Sultan himself saw the blood of the Greeks flowing like a river. The Turkish occupation lasted 390 years, 390 difficult years under the oppressive yoke of the conqueror.

The Greeks, because they had resisted, were tortured, deprived of their property and driven out of the walled city, which was now inhabited only by Turks and Jews. In spite of persecution, considerable numbers of Rhodians took part in the struggle for national lib-

pp. 38 - 39

Part of the Governor's Palace in the New City of Rhodes. The monument in the photograph marks the spot where, in 1948 the Greek flag was raised when the rule of the Dodecanese was handed over to the Greeks. In the background is the St Nicholas tower.

eration and many became members of the Philikí Etaireía
(Society of Friends), the secret organisation set up to pro-
mote it. However, the island could not rise up in a body,
because of the constant presence of a Turkish army. In
1912, the Italians, in an effort to weaken the Turks, landed
forces on Rhodes and took it. They held it until 1943 and
then surrendered it to the Germans. It was only when Germany was defeated by the Allies that the struggle of the
people of Rhodes to achieve their liberation achieved its
goal. On 7 March 1948, all the islands of the Dodecanese
were incorporated into Greece.

Ancient Art and Culture

Rhodes, as we have seen, was for many centuries an important commercial port for the eastern Mediterranean. It thus played a significant role in the region's history, and at the height of its more prosperous periods the arts and literature - painting, sculpture, poetry, philosophy, astronomy, physics, geography - flourished to a remarkable extent. After the founding of the city of Rhodes, the whole of the island's artistic life was concentrated here. At the same time, it attracted foreign artists to settle on Rhodes.

Examples of Rhodian painting in ancient times have not, unfortunately, survived. Nevertheless, the historical sources supply a wealth of information about the painters of Rhodes. Thus we know that the great Ephesian painter Parrasius (fifth century BC) and Protogenes from Cyanos in Caria (fourth century BC) worked on the island, drawing their inspiration from Greek mythology.

p. 41 ▶

The Victory of Samothrace was dedicated by the Rhodians in the Sanctuary of the Cabeiri on the island of Samothrace to commemorate their victory over Antigonus III in 190 BC, and is one of the most important creations of Rhodian sculpture of the Hellenistic age (Louvre).

About pottery we have even more information. This is an art which has been cultivated on Rhodes from Mycenaean times down to the present day; examples can be seen today in the city's Archaeological Museum. In the seventh and sixth centuries BC, when this art was at its zenith, Rhodes was the only place whose pottery could rival that of Corinth. Characteristic of this period are the vessels in the style which depicted wild goats, deer and griffins, alternating with chains of anthemia and lotus blossoms, and in the 'Fikeloura' style, decorated with partridges in the central band, between plant designs. Sculpture was an art for which Rhodes was particularly famous. Instead of marble, the Rhodian sculptors used limestone coated with mortar. In Hellenistic times the independent 'school' of art of Rhodes was

one of the most important in the Greek world and the most important in the East. At this time, there were 130 foreign artists, drawn from 50 different Greek cities, working on the island. Among the most famous of the sculptors who worked on Rhodes were Bryaxis the Athenian (mid fourth century BC) and Lysippus of Sicyon, who produced a four-horse chariot of the god Helios. Lysippus's pupil Chares of Lindos was the creator of the Colossus of Rhodes, while Boethus (second century BC) adorned the sanctuary of Lindian Athena with his works. Some items from the studios of Rhodes enjoy world-wide fame: the Sleeping Eros in bronze, now in the Metropolitan Museum in New York, and the Victory of Samothrace (in the Louvre), which was a votive offering of the Rhodians to the sanctuary of the Great Gods on Samothrace to commemorate their victory over Antiochus III in 190 BC. Another famous example of the work of the Rhodian school of sculpture is the Laocöon group (second century BC) in the Vatican Museum, attributed to the sculptors Agesander, Polydorus, and Athenodorus.

Apart from being a centre for the plastic arts, Rhodes was the home of many men of letters, such as Pisander of Cameiros (sixth century BC), the poet Cleobulus of Lindos (sixth century BC), one of the 'Seven Sages' of antiquity and tyrant of his native city, the poet Timocreon of Ialysos (fifth century BC), author of a collection of poems entitled Melika, and Anaxandrides of Cameiros (fourth century BC), who wrote comedies and dithyrambs.

The Alexandrian poet Apollonius (third century BC), known as Apollonius of Rhodes, is so called because he spent all his life, or the greater part of it, on the island. Other intellectuals who settled here include the philosopher Aristippus of Cyrene, a pupil of Socrates, and the Athenian orator Aeschines (fourth century BC), who founded a school of rhetoric on the island. Many Rhodians distinguished themselves in the field of philosophy, such as Eudemus of Rhodes, who introduced the Peripatetic school of philosophy on Rhodes, and Panaetius of Cameiros (second century BC).

Rhetoric, grammatical studies, geography, physics, mathematics, astronomy, and medicine also flourished on the island.

p. 42

A copy of the famous Laocöon group in the Palace of the Grand Masters in Rhodes. The original is in the Vatican Museum in Rome. This is one of the most famous works of the Hellenistic 'baroque' and is attributed to the Rhodian sculptors Agesander, Polydorus, and Athenodorus. According to the myth, Laocöon was a priest of Troy. He tried to persuade the Trojans not to allow the Trojan Horse within their city, but before he was able to do this, two huge snakes, sent by the gods hostile to Troy, strangled him and his sons while they were sacrificing at an altar.

The Colossus of Rhodes

The Colossus of Rhodes was, of course, in its time one of the 'Seven Wonders of the World'. There has been much discussion of its 'colossal' size and the issue of where exactly it must have stood, but these questions cannot be answered with certainty, given that not a single fragment of it has survived. The only evidence of its existence are the descriptions of travellers who came to Rhodes to see it.

The Rhodians put up the Colossus to honour their protector Helios, the sun-god, after the unsuccessful attempt of Demetrius Poliorcetes to take their city in 305/4 BC. The cost was met from the sale of the siege engines which Demetrius had left behind on the island and which realised the sum of 300 talents, the equivalent of approximately three billion present-day drachmas.

The statue was commissioned from the sculptor Chares of Lindos and took some 12 years to complete. According to the ancient sources, the statue's limbs were constructed in sections. Construction started off from a marble base, to which the feet and ankles were fixed. The remaining parts of the body were gradually added, those already in place having earth piled up against them, so that work could be continued at ground level. It seems, then, that a hill of earth must gradually have been built up round the statue, which by the time it was finished must have had a height of some 30 metres. The head of the Colossus was in all probability ringed with rays, in the manner of an earthenware head of Helios which is in the Rhodes Museum. In his right hand the god held a torch, used as a landmark by mariners. Most of the information which we have about the stance of the statue is derived from writers and representations dating from the Byzantine age and is, of course, adapted to Byzantine ideas of aesthetics.

Various hypotheses have been put forward about where the

p. 47 ▶

The Colossus of Rhodes.

statue stood. According to one view, it was sited at the entrance to the harbour, so that ships passed beneath its parted legs. According to others, it stood in the precinct of the Temple of Helios, which is to be identified with the site on which the Palace of the Grand Master stands today.

There are also many theories as to the size of the Colossus. Travellers who visited Rhodes inform us that it that it had a height of 31 - 32 metres. According to their descriptions, there was room for 12 men on its chest, a man could stand upright in its head, its nose was 30 cms long, and a fingernail 15 cms. The Roman writer Pliny, who saw the statue on Rhodes in 77 BC, tells us that one could only just put one's arms round its thumb. The impression which the statue made upon the ancient world is reflected in one of the dialogues of Lucian. He tells us that Menippus, on his way up into the sky, could make out the earth only

because the Colossus of Rhodes and the Lighthouse of Alexandria were visible up to cloud level.

The Colossus stood in its original position for a total of 56 years, until, in 227/6 BC it was demolished by an earthquake. Although the Rhodians actually got together the funds necessary for re-erecting it, in the end they did not put it back in position, heeding an oracle which warned them that this would cause many disasters for the people of the island. Thus it remained for some 800 years exactly as it had fallen, a sight to be seen for visitors to Rhodes.

The fact that the statue remained fallen but untouched for so many centuries, even though the bronze of which it was made was valuable, shows the pride of the Rhodians in their island's creation. In 653 AD, the Moabite Arabs, who had conquered the island, sold its bronze members to a Jewish merchant, who is said to have needed 900 camels to carry it off.

pp. 48- 49

View of the entrance to Mandraki, with the St Nicholas tower. According to the traditional view, which has, however, been called into question in recent times, the Colossus of Rhodes straddled the entrance to the harbour with its feet where the two bronze deer now stand.

Vernacular Architecture

p. 50

Decorative motif from a traditional Rhodian house.

p. 51 ►

Typical door in the village oof Koskinou. The shades of colour and the elaborate decoration create a harmonious result which lends a picturesque appearance to the ekistic unit.

The ekistic picture presented by any location is indissolubly bound up with the morphology of the terrain, its geographical position, and its history. Thus, the most important settlement on Rhodes, its capital, developed on its northern coast, in a key position for maritime communication in the area. The rest of the settlements which are of importance today are very close to the capital, and on the road axes which linked the ancient cities of Lindos, Ialysos, and Cameiros.

Today, it is the northern part of the island which is of most tourist interest, while the rest of it contains settlements of some importance from the point of view of planning and architectural form.

The settlements of Rhodes can be divided into coastal and inland. Those on the coast, such as Rhodes and Lindos, are usually built in amphitheatre form on some natural harbour, as a rule looking out to sea, as in the case of Lindos. The history of the coastal settlements goes back to antiquity; Rhodes and Lindos in particular were major commercial centres, their influence extending over the whole region, and with a history which continues into the Middle

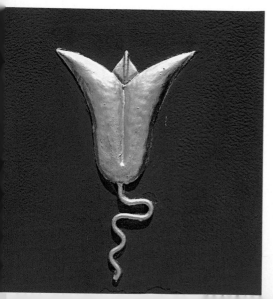

Ages. When all the other coastal centres were transferred into the interior, Rhodes and Lindos became strong fortresses.

The development of the inland settlements was the result of the need of the inhabitants to protect themselves against pirate raids in the Byzantine period and after the fall of the city to the Turks.

Thus the inhabitants of the coastal villages deserted their homes and chose sites which were not visible from the sea and the main roads, including the sides of mountains or hills, small valleys or plains, or areas near rivers, on which to build their new villages, most of which were fortified. In order to protect themselves from pirates, the Rhodians also built castles into which to retire in the event of a raid, and tower-houses, the latter being mostly on the coast of the island.

The materials used in the building of these settlements were those which can be found in abundance on the island: stone, earth and wood.

The types of houses to be encountered on Rhodes took shape in accordance with the everyday needs of the residents, their aesthetic sense, the climatic conditions, and the landscape. The can be divided into the following six types: - **The farm or single-roomed house of the common people**, which housed the less prosperous families. This consisted of a single room, usually rectangular, which served all the needs of the family: here it worked, ate, slept and entertained guests. Wood was used for the roofing, while the floor was either of trodden earth or paved with pebbles. These pebbles,

p. 52

Typical pebble floor with geometrical and plant designs in the courtyard of a Rhodian house.

called *'chochlákia'* in the local dialect, are black and white and, more rarely, red and green. The single-roomed house gradually took on more complex forms. Its single space continued to provide the living-quarters, but various ancillary items, such as the kitchen, stables and oven, were built round it.

  - **The semi-urban house.** This is to be met with in areas where the inhabitants were engaged in trade and shipping and, consequently, were more well-to-do. Houses of this type constitute a variation on the developed form of the type described above. Often they were of two storeys and richly decorated inside and out. The

p. 53

The village of Lindos with the Church of Our Lady (fourteenth century) in the centre.

courtyard was separated from the road by a wall and was entered through a gateway.

p. 55 ▶

Traditional yard gate at a house in the village of Koskinou.

p. 54

Old mansion, Lindos. Note the distinctly Gothic decoration of the facade, with doors and windows with pointed arches.

- **Mansions at Lindos.** The various conquerors who passed through this place, one of the most ancient settlements on the island, have left their mark on the architecture of its houses. Most of the mansions *(archontiká)* of Lindos were built in the early seventeenth century and took on features from the traditional island, Byzantine, medieval, and even Arab styles. A typical feature is the rich decoration both of the interiors (painted ceilings) and of the facades and the courtyards, which are paved with pebbles.

- **'Towers'.** These are buildings which go back to the period of the Knights of St John. They can be seen in the medieval town of Rhodes and in the countryside, in the Trianta area. They are two-storey buildings, constructed in dressed stone and with embrasures at roof level.

- **Turkish houses.** The settling of Turks on the island, naturally enough, influenced its architecture. The new type of house which appeared was, of course, influenced by the East; its interior was sparsely furnished, but rich in decoration. Another typical feature of the Turkish house is the *'sachnisí'*, a wooden trellis covering the balconies and windows in the facade.

- **The houses of Marasia.** The type of house to be encountered in Marasia is oblong, usually of a single storey, and known as *'makrynária'*.

The City of Rhodes

The monuments of the city of Rhodes, incontrovertible witnesses to a history which begins somewhere at the end of the fifth century BC, help us to gain a picture, even if sometimes a dim one, of this city in each of the periods of its history: antiquity, Byzantine times, the Middle Ages, Turkish rule. These successive testimonies together with its present go to make up the enchanting image of the city of Rhodes as it is today.

a. Ancient Rhodes

Ancient Rhodes was founded in 408 BC, as a result of the joint decision taken by the three major city-states of the island - Cameiros, Ialysos, Lindos - to set up a single city in common. The spot chosen as the most suitable site was the most northerly point of the island, from which the shipping in the eastern Aegean could be monitored. The city was named the 'deme of the Rhodians'. It was built on the Hippodamian system and was famous for its town planning. Its streets were broad and were arranged vertically and horizontally to form right angles with each other. We learn from ancient authors that it was adorned with large numbers of temples and statues. It had five **harbours**, of which the position of three has been identified, while any trace of the other two has been lost. One of these is to be identified with what is today the large commercial harbour. Another was the naval harbour, which occupied the Mandraki area and could be closed with a chain when the city was threatened by an enemy

p. 59 ➤

Entrance to Mandraki. Archaeological research has revealed that this was the site of one of the five harbours of ancient Rhodes.

attack. The third was at the Akantia harbour.

Many of the streets of the later medieval city followed the routes of their ancient predecessors. For example, the Street of the Knights coincided with an ancient street which started out from the Temple of Helios and led to the large harbour. It is considered likely that the **Temple of the Sun** stood on roughly the same spot which is to-day occupied by the Palace of the Grand Masters. On the northern edge of the large harbour there was a **temple dedicated to Aphrodite**. The remains of this temple which have come to light indicate a date in the third century BC. To the west of this point were shipyards.

The ancient city was walled. Its **wall** included the acropolis, which was unfortified and was on the southwestern side of the city, on the Ayios Stefanos or **Monte Smith** hill. The five harbours were protected by their own special fortifications. The walled city occupied roughly the same area as the present-day city and had an area of

p. 60

The small theatre on the acropolis of ancient Rhodes (Monte Smith), now restored.

approximately 15 square kms. When its prosperity was at its height, the city's population reached 60,000 - 100,000.

The high-point in the history of the ancient city of Rhodes came in the third and second centuries BC, when it was the most important centre of entrepot trade in the eastern Mediterranean. Archaeological digs have brought to light the stadium, the theatre and temples, which were on the acropolis, and the foundations of buildings, roads, underground drainage and water-supply networks and parts of the ancient fortifications.

On the northern part of the acropolis of ancient Rhodes, the **ruins of the Temple of Athena Polias** have survived. To the south and east of the temple, structures dug out of the earth have come to light. These buildings, which have a connection with the city's underground aqueduct, have been called **'Nymphaea',** since it is believed that they were dedicated to the worship of the Nymphs. To the south-east of the Nymphaea and the

p. 61

Panoramic view of the New City of Rhodes with Mandraki and the commercial harbour, as seen from Monte Smith. In the foreground is the Temple of Pythian Apollo on Monte Smith.

Temple of Athena, a **small theatre** has been excavated
and completely reconstructed. Only three seats in the
front row are the originals. The theatre's small size (it had
only 800 seats) shows that it was not the city's main theatre, but a place used for musical and other performances
in honour of Apollo, or even for the speeches of orators.

To the south-east of the theatre, the **stadium** of the
ancient city, dating from the second century BC, has been
discovered. This too has been restored and only a few of
the tiers of seats in the sphendone are ancient. East of the
stadium was the **gymnasium**, of which little has remained.

The highest point of the acropolis, to the west, was occupied by the **Temple of Pythian Apollo**, which was approached by a large stairway. Three of the temple's
columns, supporting a part of its cornice, have been restored.

To the south-west of the stadium, tombs have been
found, but the city's **cemeteries** (fourth and third century BC) are near Rodini, the most important of all the sur-
viving tombs being the so-called Tomb of the Ptolemies.
Tombs have also been excavated in the Sgouros area, on
the road to Koskinou and in the village of Ayia Triada.

b. Byzantine Rhodes

In the Byzantine period (fourth century AD - 1309), the
city of Rhodes was capital of the Theme of Cibyra, an
important naval and military base, and the see of an Orthodox metropolitan. In the earthquake of 515 AD, it suffered severe damage and shrank to within boundaries
much smaller than those of the ancient city. Although its
resultant extent and structure are not known for certain,
it has been established that it consisted of the Byzantine
fortress and the fortified city.

To the same period belongs a large number of Early

◀ *p. 62*

*Above: The city
walls of Rhodes and
the Palace of the
Grand Masters.*

*Below: The
sanctuary apses of
the Church of Our
Lady of Burgo.*

Christain churches scattered all over the island. In the city itself, a basilica with mosaic floors of the fifth century AD has been discovered in its south-western quarter (at the point where Pavlou Mela and Cheimarras Streets meet), together with a building with mosaic floors of the same period (in Cheimarras Street), and another basilica near the new stadium.

In the thirteenth century, a period when Rhodes was ruled by the brothers Leon and Ioannes Gavalas, the Byzantine churches were built inside the castle. When the Turks invaded the island, they converted these churches into mosques in order to meet their own religious requirements.

c. The Rhodes of the Knights

After the establishment here of the Knights of St John in 1309, the city of Rhodes became the centre of the Order. Its port underwent considerable development. Pilgrims to the Holy Land used it as a staging-post on their way to Jerusalem. New buildings were put up and the fortifications were strengthened and improved, and the city thus took on a medieval character.

It was divided by an inner wall into two unequal parts, the Collachium, the smaller part, and the Chora or Burgo. The Collachium centred on the Street of the Knights and contained the Palace of the Grand Masters, the administrative centre, the Catholic Cathedral, the infirmary, the 'inns' of the various 'Tongues', the residences of the Knights, the dockyard and the arsenal. The Chora or Burgo was to the south of the Collachium. Within its walls were the residences of the various peoples who lived in the city, including the Greeks and the Jews, the market, Orthodox and Catholic churches, the synagogue, public buildings, and the barracks.

The architectural style followed during the time of the Knights can be divided into two phases. In the first (1309- 1480), the Gothic style, with some variations, was adopted. The craftsmen employed were local, with the result that their work shows certain Byzantine features.

In the second phase (1480 - 1522), which began with the first siege of the city by the Turks (1480) and the catastrophic earthquake of 1481, the Late Gothic style, influenced by Italian Renaissance art, was followed. During this period, the damage caused by the earthquake and the siege to the public buildings and fortifications was repaired. Of all the Grand Masters, D'Aubusson was the one who concerned himself most with the strengthening of the fortifications.

The **walls** which surrounded the city had a perimeter of 4 kms and were ringed by a moat, which at many points was double. The fortifications included the wall on land, the harbour wall and the walls of the harbour moles. Each 'Tongue' was assigned a specific section of the walls to defend in the event of an enemy attack. The castle had a total of seven gates: St Paul's Gate at its northern end led to the Naillac tower at the end of the northern mole of the harbour; the D'Amboise Gate was built in 1512; the Gate of St Athanasius was on the southwestern side of the city; the Koskinou Gate, also known as the Gate of St John; the Gate of St Catherine or 'of the Mills' owed its second name to the 13 mills which stood on the mole (today only three remain); the Sea Gate in the middle of the commercial harbour, and, further north, the Harbour Gate.

From time to time, the fortifications were strengthened by the construction of towers, such as the those of Spain, of Our Lady, of St Paul (at the end of the northern mole) and of St Nicholas (at the end of the southern mole).

d. Turkish rule - Modern times

When Rhodes was taken by the hordes of Suleyman the Magnificent in 1522, the Greeks were driven out of the walled city and were forced to live outside in districts which they created and called *marásia*. The Turks, of course, on taking over the city, had no need to put up new buildings: they made use of the existing ones, adding their own features and adapting them to their needs. The churches, with the addition of a minaret, were turned into mosques, while

the houses of the Christians completely met the needs of their new occupants after the *sachnisiá* (wooden trellises covering balconies and windows) had been added. All that was built were a few mosques, three Turkish baths, and some shops and warehouses in the market. The Italians, who succeeded the Turks as rulers of the island in 1912, re-built the city, removing the additions made by the Turks. They also put up new buildings at the Mandraki harbour and around the medieval city.

pp. 66 - 67

Modern fountain, Mandraki. In the background are the statues of the deer at the entrance to the harbour, and the St Nicholas tower.

A Tour of the City of Rhodes

The Collachium - Archaeological Museum - Palace of the Grand Masters

Our first visit to the old town will take us to the Collachium, the centre of public life for the city of the Knights. Its buildings, erected during their rule, are preserved today in the form which they took after their restoration by the Italians during their rule of the island.

We enter the Old City through the **Gate of Liberty**, which is on the northern side of the wall. This gate is of a later date: it was constructed under Italian rule. We find ourselves immediately in **Symi Square**. In front of us are the ruins of the **ancient Temple of Aphrodite**, a work of the third century BC. On the south of Symi Square is **Arghyrokastrou Square**, which contains, on its eastern side, the house of **Hassan Bey**, a mansion of the late eighteenth and early nineteenth century.

West of the house of Hassan Bey stands the **Inn of Auvergne**, which dates from the fifteenth century. The city had an 'inn' for each of the Tongues - large buildings with ancillary outbuildings, their size depending upon the number of knights they provided for.

The members of the Order did not live in the inns, but in houses within the Collachium. The inns were used by the members of each Tongue as places in which to dine together and discuss matters of common interest. On occasion, they also served to provide hospitali-

p. 69 ►

The most impressive monument of the Rhodes of the Knights is undoubtedly the Palace of the Grand Masters, which stands out for the strength and luxury of its construction.

p. 70

The entrance to the new Hospital of the Knights, which today houses the Rhodes Archaeological Museum.

ty for distinguished visitors to the island. On the south side of the Inn of Auvergne there is an inscription on a marble plaque with the name of the Grand Master Guy de Blanchefort and the date 1507.

The building to the west of the Inn today houses the **Library of the Historical and Archaeological Insti-**

tute. It would seem that this building, one of the oldest in the city, was originally used as the infirmary of the Knights. It was probably built in the time of the Grand Master De Pins (1355 - 1365).

ARCHAEOLOGICAL MUSEUM OF RHODES

p. 71

We continue south, through Megalou Alexandrou Square, to **Museum Square**. On its western side is the main entrance to the new **Hospital of the Knights**, which today houses the **Archaeological Museum of Rhodes**. The Hospital was one of the most important buildings of the city of the Knights. Over the pointed arch of its main entrance there is a marble plaque depicting two angels holding the coat-of-arms of the Grand Master Fluvian. Below, an inscription informs us that the Grand Master gave 10,000 gold florins towards the erection of the building, which began on 15 July 1440 under the Grand Master De Lastic (1437 - 1454) and was completed in 1489, when D'Aubusson was Grand Master (1476 - 1503). This plaque is built into the outside of the central apse of the Hospital's chapel, which is exactly above the entrance.

One kouros found in the Cameiros region and dating from the sixth century BC. He shows strong island influence.

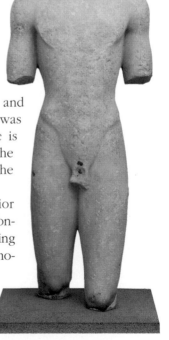

The building consists of a large interior courtyard surrounded by a two-storey colonnade. On display here are a marble lion dating from Hellenistic times, an Early Christian mosaic showing birds and fishes, and piles of stone and iron missiles from the sieges of Demetrius Poliorcetes and of the Turks, respectively. On the south

side of the central courtyard is another, smaller, one, with mosaics.

On the left of the entrance a broad staircase leads to the upper storey of the Hospital. The eastern side of the building is taken up by a rectangular hall, divided lengthwise by an arch supported on seven columns. This contained the beds of the patients; on its south side there was a fireplace, while on the eastern and western sides there were recesses in the walls for the isolation of the sick. At present, tombstones of the period of the Knights and a marble sarcophagus of the Classical period used for the burial of the Grand Master Pierre de Corneillan are on show here.

◄ *p. 72*

The grave stele of Calliarista, of the fourth century BC. The dead woman is shown seated, following the models of Attic art. Her slave stands in front of her and offers her a box containing jewellery.
(Timarista Room).

p. 73

Two small statues of Asclepius and Hygeia. They date from the third century.

p. 74

A. The great hall for
the patients in the
Hospital of the
Knights. It now
contains gravestones
from the period of
the Knights.

On the west side, a large hall served as a refectory for the staff of the Hospital. This is divided into smaller areas and contains exhibits dating from the Archaic to the Roman period. Among these are grave steles, the torsos from Archaic *kouroi*, and a number of Classical sculptures. Of particular beauty, and influenced by the art of Phidias, is the stele of Crito and Timarista, which was carved at Cameiros in the late fifth century BC. The stele, of a height of two metres, shows the dead Timarista receiving her daughter Crito in her embrace.

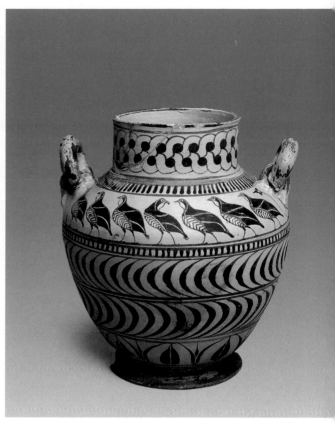

Of interest also is a *perirrhanterion* (vessel used for ritual lustrations) of the seventh century BC, whose bowl is supported by three women standing on the body of a lion, thus suggesting dominance over wild nature. These galleries lead to a hanging garden, which is adorned with grave steles and sculptures.

In the galleries which we come to next, three statues of the goddess Aphrodite stand out among the Hellenistic sculptures. In one of these, the goddess is shown life-size in the modest stance which has been

p. 74

B. Rhodian wine-pourer with a three-leafed mouth. Seventh century BC, from Cameiros.

p. 75

Typical vessel in the 'Fikeloura' style of the sixth century BC.

p. 76

A. *Marble head of an athlete, found on the slopes of the acropolis of Rhodes. It dates from the Hellenistic period.*

B. *Headless statue of a nymph. It dates from the Late Hellenistic period.*

C. *Headless statue of a nymph or Aphrodite bending, with her right foot on a rock. A typical example of Late Hellenistic 'rococo'.*

p. 77 ➤

The famous statuette of the Aphrodite of Rhodes, of the first century BC. It is considered to be a reworking of a sculpture by the Bythinian Daedalsas (third century BC). The goddess is shown, with the utmost artistic skill, taking her bath.

called 'Venus Pudica' (third century BC), while in another (second century BC) she rests her foot on a rock. It is easy for the visitor to miss a small marble statue depicting Aphrodite bathing. Kneeling on a rock, the goddess lifts her hair in her hands (Venus Bathing or the Aphrodite of Rhodes - first century BC).

p. 78

Headless statue of a seated god, most probably Zeus. (Room of the Lesser Aphrodite).

This little masterpiece is thought to be a re-working of a sculpture by the Bythinian sculptor Daedalsas, who lived in the third century BC. Nearby we can see a highly expressive earthernware head of the sun-god Helios of the second half of the second century BC, a large number of statues of nymphs, a statue of Artemis-Hecate, a headless statue of a Muse, a head of an athlete, and two statuettes of Asclepius and Hygeia of the third century BC. In the next gallery to this there is a marble head which has been identified as a Roman copy of a portrait of the poet Menander.

The remaining galleries of the Museum in the upper storey around the courtyard contain important examples of the ceramics produced by Rhodes from the Geometric to the Classical period, while in the colonnade there are grave steles and altars from the Hellenistic and Roman periods.

On the eastern side of Museum

p. 79 ►

The grave stele of Crito and Timarista is one of the most important exhibits in the Rhodes Archaeological Museum (in the room of the same name). It is a superb work of the fifth century BC and is strongly influenced by Attic art of the time of Pheidias.

p. 80

A. Small head in porphyrite stone showing Silenus or Bacchus, probably drunk. An interesting work of the Middle Hellenistic period. (Great Aphrodite Room).

B. Statue of a young child, a fine work of the Late Hellenistic period. (Great Aphrodite Room).

p. 81 ▶

A. Marble head of a woman from the Nymphaeum of Rhodes, dating from the Late Hellenistic period. (Great Aphrodite Room).

B. Statuette of child lifting its cloak, a typical example of Late Hellenistic 'rococo'. (Room of the Lesser Aphrodite).

C. Cult statue of Aphrodite, which gave its name to the room of the Museum in which it is exhibited (Great Aphrodite Room). It was brought up from the bottom of the sea near the Grand Hotel, the site of one of the ancient harbours of Rhodes. The statue belongs to the so-called 'Venus pudica' type, in which the goddess attempts to cover her breasts with her right hand and to hold up her garment, which has slipped down, with her left. In this case, the hands are missing.

p. 82

Marble statue of Zeus from Cameiros, Middle Hellenistic period. (Room of the Lesser Aphrodite).

Square is the **house of Guy de Melay**, which now houses the National Bank. Next to it, on the north-east of the Square, is the **Inn of England**, which has on its northern side the coat-of-arms of the Tongue and the devices of three knights.

East of Museum Square, we come to the ruins of the **Church of Our Lady of the Castle**, an old Byzantine church (building began in the eleventh or twelfth century) in the shape of a cross with added Gothic features, given that it was completed by the Knights. It has Byzantine (fourteenth century) and Frankish wall-paintings. Our Lady of the Castle was the Roman Catholic cathedral.

Later, the Turks were to convert it into the so-called Enterum Mosque.

Exactly opposite, to the west of the church, is the beginning of the **Street of the Knights**, the main street of the medieval city. It is as much as six metres wide and at two points is arched over.

To left and right are the inns of the remaining Tongues of the Order. First on our right is the **Inn of Italy**, while on the left is the northern side of the new Hospital.

The building which has been identified as the Inn of Italy is relatively small for the number of members of the Tongue of Italy. Over the entrance there is a marble relief with the coat-of-arms of the Grand Master Del Carretto (1513 - 1521). Next door is the **Inn of France**, the finest building in the city of the Knights. Its facade is adorned with the heraldic devices of the Tongue of France, the Grand Master D'Aubusson

(1476 - 1503), and the last Grand Master, Villiers de l'Isle Adam (1521 - 1534). To the north-west of the inn there is a building called the house of **Prince Djem**. Tradition relates that it was here that Prince Djem, the exiled brother of the Sultan Bayezid and pretender to the throne, was entertained by the Grand Master D'Aubusson.At the end of a little street which begins at this point and is flanked by a colonnade stands the single-aisled **Gothic Church of St Demetrius**.

On the left-hand side of the Street of the Knights, west of the Hospital, stands the **house of Diomede de Villaragout**, a fifteenth-century building with a rectan-

p. 83

The main street of medieval Rhodes was the Street of the Knights, which survives in good condition today. The Street of the Knights is flanked by interesting buildings, now restored, which belonged to the Knights and which today introduce the visitor into an atmosphere of the Middle Ages.

gular inner courtyard. Further west, as the street becomes uphill, we have on our left the **Inn of Spain** and on our right the **Inn of Provence**.

Over the portal to the Inn of Provence, which is in many ways similar to that of France, there is a marble relief bearing the coats-of-arms of the Tongue, of France, of the Grand Master Del Carretto, and of the knight Francis Flote.

The Inn of Spain, which accommodated the Tongues of Catalonia and Castille, is simpler in form than the other inns; it bears the coat-of-arms of the Grand master Fluvian. On the same side of the road are the remains of the **Church of St John of the Collachium**, built in the early fourteenth century and dedicated to the patron saint of the Order. A three-aisled church in the Gothic style, it was used for the burial of Grand Masters. A large part of the church and the colonnade which linked it with the Palace of the Grand Masters (on the right of the street) were destroyed in 1856 when a gunpowder magazine which had been in the basement of the church's bell-tower since 1522 was struck by lightning. The Church of the Annunciation at Mandraki is a copy of the Church of St John of the Collachium, built by the Italians. The site of the Church of St John was occupied by a Turkish school, while the colonnade has been to a large extent restored

p. 84

The interior of Our Lady of the Castle, a Byzantine church of the eleventh or twelfth century, completed in the time of the Knights and showing Gothic features.

THE PALACE OF THE GRAND MASTERS

To the north of the Street of the Knights, the **Palace of the Grand Masters**, the largest building of the medieval city, stands in all its grandeur. The Palace too was badly damaged by the explosion of the powder magazine of St John, but was restored by the Italians, who paved the floors with mosaics of the Hellenistic, Roman and Byzantine periods, mostly brought from Cos. The Palace was originally built in the fourteenth century.

It was impressively fortified and had underground storerooms where the Knights kept ammunition and foodstuffs in order to be able to deal effectively with enemy attacks. After the island was taken by the Turks

p. 85

The grand staircase leading to the upper floor of the Palace of the Grand Masters.

in 1522, it was converted into a prison. Before its destruction in 1856, it had already suffered serious damage as a result of the earthquake of 1851.

The entrance to the castle is imposing. On the left and right there are two semi-circular towers with battlements. The large rectangular inner courtyard with the arches is decorated with Roman statues. The ceilings of the rooms are of wood, often supported on rows of columns, while the floors are. paved with coloured marble.Visitors reach the first floor by a grand marble staircase. The principal rooms here are as follows:

- The room with the trophy of the Mithridatic Wars, which dates from the first century BC and comes from the cemetery of the ancient city of Rhodes. The statue stands on a marble base of the Hellenistic period and is decorated with relief figures of the god Dionysus and Maenads. The floor is adorned with mosaics of the Late Roman and Early

p. 89

The entrance to the Palace of the Grand Masters. The strong towers and ramparts which surround it are particularly striking. The Palace was not only a residence for the Grand Master, but an important stronghold, essential for the defence of the city.

Christian period, all from Cos. The wooden seats in this room are from Western Europe and date from the sixteenth century.

- The room with the statue of Laocöon and his sons. This complex is a copy of a Roman work of the first century BC which is now in the Vatican Museum and was carved by Agesander, Athenodorus, and Polydorus of Rhodes.

Here too the floor is decorated with mosaics of the Late Hellenistic period from Cos. The wooden table and chairs are of the sixteenth century, while the two wooden chests date from the eighteenth.

- The room with the mosaic of Medusa. This too is

p. 90

The chapel of the Palace of the Grand Masters.

from Cos and is a work of the second century BC. A collection of Chinese vases is on display in recesses in the walls.

- The room with the three pointed cross vaults. At their meeting-point they have symbols of the lictors of ancient Rome. The floor has two mosaics from Cos: one of these, of the Late Hellenistic period, depicts a variety of fishes and shellfish, while the other shows birds among geometric motifs and dates from the Early Christian period (first half of the sixth century BC). The wooden chests are of the sixteenth century and come from Western Europe.

p. 91

The grand staircase leading to the upper floor of the Palace of the Grand Masters.

- The room with the tiger mosaic. Part of the floor

of this room is occupied by a mosaic which shows the figure of a tiger ready to attack and another, of the Early Christian period, with geometric designs.

- The room which was used as an office of the Italian governor of the Dodecanese under Italian rule. This room too has three pointed cross vaults. Immediately below the second of these there is a mosaic floor from Cos, dating from the second half of the fifth century AD. It shows twelve circles containing ducks, trees and vases. The furniture (chairs, a desk, chests, *candelieri*) is of the sixteenth century.

- The room with the column capitals. Two rows of columns with Theodosian capitals divide the room into three aisles. In all probability it was this room which the Knights used for their meetings.

The centre of the floor is adorned with a large, rectangular mosaic of the second half of the fifth century

p. 92
_____

The room with the trophy from the Mithridatic Wars. It has mosaic floors brought from Cos.

p. 93

A. The room which served as the office of the Governor of the Dodecanese under Italian rule. The mosaic on the floor comes from Cos (fifth century AD).

B. The room with the mosaic of Medusa. The mosaic on the floor comes from Cos and dates from the second century AD.

BC with complex decorative designs. This mosaic is from the Basilica of St John on Cos. In the recesses of the wall are two *candelieri* of the seventeenth century in the form of angels.

- The room with the mosaic showing a thyrsus, a work of the second half of the first century BC. This time the mosaic is from Rhodes itself.

The chandelier which hangs from the ceiling is of Murano glass.

- The room with the lantern. On one of the walls of this room there is a wooden lantern which is supported on the wall with a hand.

The floor has a mosaic from Cos dating from the sec-

p. 94

The room with the mosaic of the Nine Muses (first century AD).

ond half of the fifth century AD.

- The room with the dolphins. The floor of this oblong room has a mosaic from Cos of the Late Hellenistic period. Round the edge dolphins are shown swimming, while the middle is occupied by the figure of a large fish.

After the room with the dolphins, a marble staircase leads to the storey above and from there to a corridor whose floor is made up of a series of mosaics. The first shows a warrior defending himself against an attacking tiger. This is a work of the Late Hellenistic period and is also from Cos. The second is made up of geometric designs, while the third shows Poseidon fight-

The room with the mosaic showing a nymph on a seahorse.

p. 96

Mosaic floor of the first century AD, with busts of the Nine Muses, in the room of the same name.

p. 97 ➤

Mosaic floor from Cos, dating from the second half of the fifth century AD, in the room which was used as an office of the Italian governor of the Dodecanese.

ing the Giant Polybotus.

- The Eros room. The mosaic in this room is of the Late Hellenistic period. It is from Cos and shows, in vivid colours, Eros fishing.

- The room with the mosaic of the Nine Muses. The floor is dominated by a mosaic in its centre which is of the Late Hellenistic period and shows busts of the Nine Muses. The furniture and the tapestries date from the sixteenth century.

The Chora or Burgo

p. 99 ➤

Ippokratous Square is one of the most central points of the city of Rhodes and bustles with life all day long. In the background is the Palace of the Castellan (a commercial court under the rule of the Knights), which today houses the Library of Rhodes.

p. 98

View of the Old Town with its typical alleyways, roofed by stone arches.

In this part of the medieval city we shall visit a large number of churches built in the Byzantine period and in the time of the Knights and public buildings such as the Palace of the Castellan, the 'Admiralty', and the Hospice of St Catherine.

We begin our visit from **Ippokratous Square**, at the north-eastern end of which is the **Palace of the Castellan**. Its ground floor today houses the Library of Rhodes. On the south-western side of the building, a wide outside staircase leads to a rectangular flat roof which looks out over Ippokratous Square.

On one side of the roof, a door with a carved marble frame opens on to a large window divided into four by a marble cross. On the wall there is a marble relief with the coat-of-arms of the Grand Master D'Amboise and the date 1507. The Castellan building seems to have been used as the commercial court of the island and was a meeting-point for merchants.

As we leave the Castellan building in a south-eastely direction, we come to the **Square of the Jewish Martyrs**. On

p. 100

Above: The fountain in the Square of the Jewish Martyrs.

Below: A traditional-style coffee shop in Sokratous Street.

the northern side of this is a building known as the **Admiralty**. This was probably built towards the end of the fifteenth and in the early sixteenth centuries and must have been the residence of the Greek (i.e., Orthodox) Metropolitan of Rhodes. The facade of the building bears the Latin inscription: *Pax huic domui et omnibus habitantibus in ea* ('Peace be in this house and all those dwelling herein'). The same inscription translated into Greek is to be found on the northern

wall of the inner courtyard.

On the wall above the central portal is a plaque bearing an unknown coat-of-arms which has been incorporated into the masonry. Further to the east, on the southern side of Aristotelous Street, is the Knights' **Hospice of St Catherine**.

This was managed by the Tongue of Italy and was built in the fourteenth century by the Admiral of the Order Domenico d'Allemagna. It served as a guest-house

p. 101

Ippokratous Square by night takes on a 'phantasmagorical' appearance, as the lights of the shops create striking contrasts with the city's monuments.

for the Knights. Near the Gate of St Catherine is the Church of **St Panteleimon**, now a parish church, which was built to commemorate the victory over the Turks of 1481. From the Square of the Jewish Martyrs, Dimosthenous and Perikleous Streets start out. There are two Byzantine churches in these streets, known, respectively, as the **Dulapli Cami** and the **Il Mihrab Cami** as a result of their conversion into mosques by the Turks.

We can return to Ippokratous Square by way of Sokratous Street, which is today the busiest street in the Old City, though, lined with its old low houses, it has lost none of its picturesqueness. The end of Sokratous Street is dominated by the **Mosque of Suleyman**, which stands on the site of the Byzantine Church of the Holy Apostles. In the garden there is a fountain of the sixteenth century. Sokratous Street is succeeded by Orfeos Street, at the beginning of which is the famous **'Clock'**, a three-storey tower, which was a gift of Tahti Pasha to the Turks of the city.

It has been converted into a bar and provides a panoramic view in the direction of the harbour. Opposite the Clock stands the building of the **Turkish Library**, founded in 1794 by Havuz Ahmet Aga. Among the rare manuscripts which this contains are an illuminated Koran of 1540 and a chronicle of the siege of 1522. In the same area, in Apollonion Street, there is four-apsed church of the fourteenth century.

This came into the possession of the Franciscans in the fifteenth century and was decorated with Gothic features. Under the Turks, it was converted into a theological college, known as the **Hurmali Medrese**.

There are two other Byzantine churches nearby, in Ippodamou Street. These two were used by the Turks as mosques and have continued to be known as the **Takkeci Cami** and the **Cadi Mescid**. At the south end of Ippodamou Street, near the Gate of St Athanasius, there is a single-aisled Byzantine church with the same dedica-

p. 102

The main street of the Old Town of Rhodes is Sokratous Street, full of shops and strolling visitors. In the background is the Mosque of Suleyman.

tion, but, having also had the same fate as the other churches, known as **Bab-u-Mestud**.

Parallel with Ippodamou Street is Ayiou Fanouriou Street, one of the most colourful in the Old City. It contains the Byzantine **Church of St Phanurius**, built in the thirteenth century in a free cross shape and decorated with very interesting wall-paintings.

p. 105 ➤

Ayiou Fanouriou Street is one of the most picturesque in the Old Town. This is where the Turkish quarter is to be found - with its paved alleys, its crossed arches, its vaulted houses and its host of minarets.

p. 104

The whole of the Old Town of Rhodes provides visitors with a unique atmosphere, taking them back to the days of old.

Here the Kavoukli Metali Cami was built under Turkish rule. Another mosque is preserved behind the Church of St Phanurius, the **Redjeb Pasha Cami**, in whose construction architectural members from ancient, Byzantine and medieval buildings were used.

The **Demirli Cami**, a large fourteenth-century church, used both in the time of the Knights and under Turkish rule, can be seen in Platonos Street, which is at right angles with Ayiou Fanouriou Street.

There are plenty of other Byzantine churches to be seen in the Old City of Rhodes, most of which today are in the form of mosques as a result of the alterations which they underwent at the hands of the Turkish conquerors. Also of considerable interest are the Turkish monuments, which give the visitor a glimpse of a different sort of architecture and blend in harmoniously

with the buildings of antiquity, of Byzantine times and of the Knights. It is precisely this multifariousness which gives the Old City its unique character and is a basic reason for the presence of large numbers of visitors at all times of the year. Behind the busy shops, restaurants, cafeterias and places of entertainment of every kind, it is easy to find a rich variety of historical monuments which reflect perfectly the glories of the city's past.

The New City

The New City of Rhodes owes its existence to the migration of the residents to outside the walls after the siege of Suleyman the Magnificent in 1522. Its development and buildings date chiefly from the time of the Italian occupation. The Italians adorned it with new buildings in the neo-Gothic and Venetian style, many of which are still standing today, giving the city a character all its own - particularly in the area of the port. Most of the activities of the island are concentrated in the modern city, which is marked by careful planning, with wide streets and a large number of parks and squares.

The highly developed tourist trade has resulted in the building of many luxury hotels, designed with a modern approach to aesthetics. It is in this part of the city that most of the places of entertainment are to be found, keeping it alive until the early hours and giving it its cosmopolitan flavour.

The **Akantia** harbour lies on the eastern side of the city of Rhodes, with the **commercial harbour**, which in antiquity was known as the Great Harbour, next to it to the west. It was in this area that in ancient times that the 'Deigma' - a richly decorated building complex used as a commercial centre - stood.

p. 109 ▶

Mandraki, with the New Market building in the foreground. In the background is the Palace of the Grand Masters.

Unfortunately, nothing has remained of this - or of the ancient Agora (marketplace), or the famous Theatre of Dionysus, which the archaeologists place near the Great Harbour. The third harbour of ancient Rhodes was the naval harbour, which has been identified with what is

now **Mandraki**, to the west of the commercial harbour. Mandraki is one of the most attractive places in the whole island and bustles with life all the year round. The picture composed by the fishing-boats, the tourist launches and the visiting yachts is enchanting, particularly if we have in mind the traidition that it was here that the Colossus stood with legs apart to control the entry of shipping.

The points at which, if the tradition is correct, the Colossus would have planted his feet, in front of the St Nicholas tower and on the mole opposite, are now occupied by **two bronze deer** on columns, which have become a kind of modern emblem of Rhodes.

Three **windmills** also stand on the St Nicholas mole, the only ones to remain of the 13 which were there in the time of the Knights, but enough to contribute to the picturesqueness of the harbour.

The greater part of the Mandraki area is taken up with the **New Market**, an imposing building dating from the time of Italian rule. Today it is a bustling centre, full of restaurants, cafés and shops, a meeting-place for visitors and locals alike.

Behind the New Market, in Rimini Square, the gardens of the Palace of the Grand Masters have been laid out to be the venue for the **'Son et Lumière'** spectacle, which every evening transports visitors back to other times.

In the same area, **itinerant artists** set up their easels every morning and produce portraits of passers-by with striking speed and fidelity. Artists also have their 'pitch' in the idyllic spot called Platanakia in Orfeos Street in the Old City, near the D'Amboise Gate.

There are buildings of great interest to be seen to the north of the harbour. The first of these is the **Church of the Annunciation**, the cathedral of Rhodes, originally built by the Italians as a cathedral dedicated to St John.

Next to it is the **Archiepiscopate** building and the

p. 111

Above: The Church of the Annunciation in the New City of Rhodes (1925). It follows the design of the old Church of St John, which was built under the rule of the Knights.

Below: The Governor's Palace in the New City.

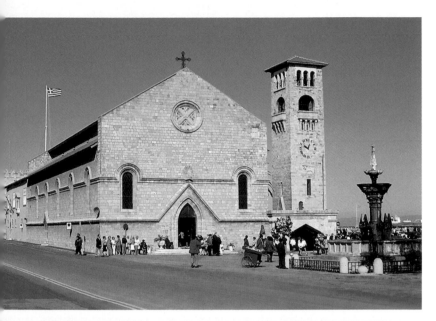

Governor's Palace, built in a mixture of Byzantine, medieval and Spanish styles. A little to the north is the **Mosque of Murad Reis**, which stands on the site of the Catholic Church of St Antony. The Mosque was built by Suleyman II, the Magnificent, and was also the site of the official Turkish cemetery. The more northerly 'arm' of the harbour at Mandraki is occupied by the **Aquarium** building. The Aquarium, one of the best of its kind, contains species from Greek and tropical waters, exhibited in 24 tanks set out in a labyrinthine arrangement. It is from this point that the extremely well organised beach, crowded with holidaymakers from May to October, starts. A few kilometres to the south of the city centre is **Rodini**, a green park with channels and ponds and containing a small zoo. A visit to Rodini, which is ideal for a carefree stroll, can be combined with seeing the so-called Tomb of Ptolemy (Hellenistic period) and the ancient cemeter-

◄ p. 112

Above: View of the New City of Rhodes.

Below: Rhodes beach, on the northern edge of the city, is every summer crowded with bathers who come to enjoy the sun and the crystal-clear water.

p. 113

The Rhodes Aquarium, one of the best of its kind in the Mediterranean. It stands next to the sea on the northern edge of the city.

ies of Rhodes, outside the walls of the Old City.

The whole of the modern city is dotted with discos, bars, pubs and places where Greek music can be heard, most of which are concentrated outside the northern part of the wall, to the west of Mandraki. Near Akti Miaouli is the Rhodes **Casino**, while the **National Theatre** in Vasilissis Olgas Square caters for theatregoers. Demonstrations of traditional dances are frequently held in the summer months in the **Traditional Dance Theatre**, which is in the Old City in Andronikou Street. Another attraction of the city of Rhodes is the great scope which it provides for shopping (it has a world-wide reputation for its perfumes and drinks and its wide variety of umbrellas). The island is also well-known for its wines - particularly for its 'KAIR' champagne. Its shops provide for the visitor's every need, and have an abundance of local products - to serve as souvenirs of a stay on the island of the Sun.

pp. 114- 115

View of Mandraki from the St Nicholas tower. The New Market and the Palace of the Grand Masters can be seen in the background. All the city's harbours, with their yachts, caïques and fishing-boats, make an attractive picture.

1st Route:

Ialysos - Butterflies - Profitis Ilias - Epta Pighes

Rhodes, with its unique charms, has so much to offer that it can satisfy even the most demanding of visitors. In this section we shall give an account of the places of interest on the island by following three basic routes.

p. 117 ➤

Very close to the city of Rhodes, on its north-western side, is the Ixia area, the site of luxury hotels. The long beach at Ixia is a favourite with summer visitors.

These routes, all of which start out from the capital, will take us to uninhabited villages which have known days of glory in the past, to the crystal-clear waters of a calm sea, refreshing in the midday heat, to villages which are small but full of life, or to the magical shade of of some cool green valley.

Following these routes will require a vehicle: car, motorbike or bus. However, there are, beyond those points which everyone can reach by these means, enchanting spots which reward those who are not daunted by the idea of a certain amount of walking. Like latter-day Robinson Crusoes, they can explore further and seek out isolated spots, the tops of hills and mountains, crowned with silent, abandoned Byzantine or medieval castles, or untrodden golden beaches which they can have entirely to themselves, to enjoy the beauty of the boundless sea.

On our first route, we shall be following the west coast of the island. We leave the city of Rhodes by Exit B, and after only 4.5 kms, we come to the charm-

ing village of **Kritika**, established in 1898 by settlers from Crete.

After 8 kms, we reach **Trianta**, a village which stands among orchards, very close to the sea. Here, the whole of the shore of the bay (approximately 10 kms) is packed with modern hotels; almost half of the hotels on the island are concentrated on this side of Rhodes. At Trianta, we turn left, thus going inland away from the sea. At a distance of 5 kms, in a dense pine wood, we reach the archaeological site of **ancient Ialysos**.

The Ialysos area, as archaeological digs have shown, was inhabited at an early date - in the Minoan period.

The buildings of the Minoan settlement, whose life began around 1550 BC, was on the southern coast of the village of Trianta. It was also here that the Mycenaeans must have settled when they came to the island. Thus Ialysos also flourished during the period of the Mycenaeans; evidence of this is provided by their cemeteries at Moschou Vounara and Makra Vounara in the foothills of Filerimos. The Mycenaeans used the mountain as a stronghold, establishing there the acropolis of Achaïa, a name which the acropolis of Ialysos retained in historical times. The discovery of cemeteries dating from the Geometric and Archaic periods (eighth - sixth

pp. 118- 119

The leafy village of Trianta, very close to the ruins of ancient Ialysos, is particularly popular with tourists. Mt Filerimos, the site of ancient Ialysos and of the monastery of the same name, dating from the time of the Knights, is in the background.

century BC) between the villages of Kremasti and Trianta has proved that the area continued to be inhabited at that time.

The large area over which these cemeteries are spread indicates that Ialysos consisted of a number of small villages scattered over the plain. The names of 11 'demes' of ancient Ialysos have been identified in inscriptions. When the unification of the Rhodians took place in 408 BC, many of the inhabitants of ancient Ialysos settled in the new city, with the result that Ialysos gradually declined in importance.

In the first century BC or AD, the mountain was called 'Ochyroma' by the geographer Strabo, while from the Middle Ages down to the present it has been called Filerimos. Its strategic position was well understood by the Byzantines, who fortified it. It was in this stronghold that in 1248 John Cantacuzene was besieged by the Ge-

p. 120

The Monastery of Filerimos, now restored, dating from the rule of the Knights. It stands among trees and has a fine view out to sea and of the village of Trianta (in the background).

noese, and it was here that the Knights of St John established themselves in 1306, before taking over the city of Rhodes, and supplemented the Byzantine fortifications. In 1522, Suleyman the Magnificent made it his headquarters.

The archaeological site of ancient Ialysos - Filerimos

A peculiarity of Filerimos is that its top does not consist of a peak, but of a 'platform' of some 600 square metres. Most of the monuments which have survived are in the easternmost part of this flat area. The archaeological site extends to a higher point of the mountain, which we can reach by following a stepped roadway flanked by cypress trees.

On the left, we can see the foundations of the Tem-

p. 121

The southern side of the restored church of the Knights at Filerimos. This is a building of special architectural interest.

ple of Athena Polias. This was in the Doric style, of limestone, amphiprostyle, with six columns on each side. It had a length of 23.50 and a width of 12.50 metres. In the northern part of the cella are the foundations of the base of a cult statue. The temple dated from Hellenistic times (third or second century BC), but the worship of Athena in this area, which went back at least to the ninth century BC, suggests the existence of an earlier temple. It is for this reason that the earthernware antefixes of gorgons' heads (fifth century BC) found here (and now in the Rhodes Archaeological Museum) have been attributed to this earlier temple, which would have been built after the Persian Wars and was somehow destroyed without leaving a trace.

The destruction of the Hellenistic temple whose remains can be seen today must have occurred in the Early Christian period, when, in the fifth or sixth century AD, an Early Christian basilica was built over the greater part of it. This basilica had three aisles, each ending in an apse. The southern aisle was built outside the line of the ancient temple. Today, remains of the baptistry, which was in the area of the apse of the southern aisle, have survived. In the centre is a dug-out font in the shape of a cross, its arms having curving ends.

The bell-tower of the Knights' church, of a much later period, whose entrance occupied the southern aisle, was built over the apse of the central aisle. When the basilica itself was destroyed is unknown. A small single-aisled domed Byzantine church must have been built over its northern aisle in Byzantine times. Then, in the first half of the fourteenth century, the Knights built a monastery and another church on the site of the Byzantine church. The attractive monastery which we can see today to the right of the ancient temple was restored by the Italians.

At a short distance to the west of the ancient temple is the underground Byzantine Chapel of St George 'Hostos', with wall-paintings of the fourteenth and fifteenth centuries in which Western influences are apparent. Opposite the entrance, Christ is depicted flanked by the Apostles Peter and Paul and other saints. The upper part of the arch is decorated with paintings showing the Blessed Virgin and Christ's Passion. To the west of the Chapel of St George 'Hostos' are the remains of the katholikon (central church) and some of the cells of the Byzantine monastery which was built here in the tenth century. The katholikon of the monastery was a small three-aisled cross-in-square church.

From the southern edge of the square on the platform begins the Way of the Cross, a road which leads to the southernmost part of the hill. It is flanked by pictures showing scenes from Christ's Passion. The view from the point where this road ends is enchanting.

The path which sets out from the south of the square leads by way of the southern side of the hill to a very well preserved and partially restored Doric limestone fountain of the fourth century BC backing on to the almost sheer hillside. This consisted of a small masonry cistern, hewn out of the rock, closed in by the back wall of the fountain. In the middle of this wall there was a small window. The wall continues left and right, forming an open Π shape, while a row of six Doric columns stands in front. Six piers spring from approximately the middle of the side walls, while two others are built into these walls. The lower part, between the piers, is closed in by parapets, thus creating an open cistern behind the colonnade of piers. On the upper part of the parapets there are the remains of lions' heads from the mouths of which the water ran. The construction must have been roofed with stone slabs, just as the floor of the fountain is paved with large slabs.

At the eastern edge of the 'platform' of Filerimos are the ruins of a fortress dating from Byzantine times and the period of the Knights. The point where the fortress stood dominates the whole area and provides a panoramic view.

At the end of our visit to the archaeological site of Ialysos, we return to the main road and continue in a westerly direction, arriving after 3 kms at **Kremasti**, a village well-supplied with trees, a kilometre from the sea, which attracts increasing numbers of visitors. Here there is a ruined Venetian fortress to be seen and good food to be had at one of the many tavernas which stand along the sea-shore among the trees. Five kms further on is **Paradeisi**, the site of the island's airport.

At this point, we leave the coast road and go inland. After some 8 kms, we reach the **Valley of the Butter-flies**, which can be visited between 8.30 in the morning and 6 in the evening. Here visitors can enjoy a delightful stroll through the green valley among the plane trees, the *Liquidambar orientalis* trees and the cool running water, which sometimes flows in streams and sometimes forms little waterfalls. There, on the trunks of the trees, from July to September, tens of thousands of butterflies of the *Callimorpha* family, charmed by the balsam produced by the *Liquidambar,* find refuge. When they close their wings, the red colour of the inside is not visible and thus they do not form a contrast with the trunks of the trees. The rhythmic sound of the water accompanies the visitor. At one point, it is in fuller flood and forms a small lake, the home, among the water lilies, of ducks and geese. Tradition has it that if the visitor who comes here for the first time throws a coin into the lake and makes a wish, this will be granted. At the point where the valley comes to an end, there is a footpath which leads to the Monastery of **Our La-**

p. 125

Two views of the Valley of the Butterflies. The spectacle of thousands of butterflies settled in the park is unique. The way in which the area has been laid out, with wooden bridges and narrow footpaths winding among little lakes, streams and waterfalls, is most attractive.

dy '**Kalopetras**', which was built in 1782 by Alexandros Ipsilantis, Prince of Wallachia. From the Monastery a marvellous view can be enjoyed together with the fresh fruit with which visitors are welcomed.

From the Valley of the Butterflies we return to the main road and travelling in a south-westerly direction, we come to **Soroni**. From there it is only 3 kms to the south to the little monastery of **St Soulas** (or 'Syllas'), which stands among pines and cypresses. In the month of July, refreshments are available; there is also spring-water and a playground. The festivities here on 29 and 30 July include horse and donkey races and attract many visitors.

After St Soulas, we travel south towards the interior of the island and after some 6 kms arrive at **Dimilia**, and then **Eleousa**; from there we can visit **Profitis Ilias** and **Fountoukli**. Returning to the main road, we travel in a south-westerly direction and after 6 kms come to **Kalavarda**. Here we start to climb the foothills of Mt Profitis Ilias, and after 8 kms reach the village of **Salako**, tucked in among the green of walnut trees. Here a spring called 'Nymfi' provides most of the water supply of the city of Rhodes. We leave this pretty village behind us and continue our climb, a further 10 kms, to the summit of the green **Mt Profitis Ilias**. Here the visitor can rest in the shade of the trees and quench his thirst at one of the two attractive hotels in the area or visit the Monastery of the Prophet Elijah and take a look at the well-preserved holiday homes built here in

p. 126

The Chapel of the Prophet Elijah on the hill of the same name (Profitis Ilias). This spot offers peace and quiet, and an exceptional view.

p. 127

Above: Epta Pighes welcomes walkers with an idyllic picture formed by the gentle waters of its springs, flowing beneath the pines and the plane trees.

Below: The hotels in the Profitis Ilias area were built by the Italians - in the Tyrolean style.

the Tyrolean style during the Italian occupation.

If you wish to continue your journey inland from Salako and visit Fountoukli, you have to travel along some 6 kms of unsurfaced road. **Fountoukli** boasts the four-apsed Byzantine Church of St Nicholas, which has fine wall-paintings of the fourteenth and fifteenth centuries.

There is spring-water in the vicinity. From Fountoukli, the road leads to the villages of **Eleousa** (3 kms) and **Archipoli** (4 kms), and from there to **Epta Pighes** (5 kms). Epta Pighes is an idyllic spot, with pines and plane trees and spring-water, which forms a small lake, making a cool place of peace and quiet. There is a restaurant-canteen in the neighbourhood.

After Epta Pighes, we follow the Kolymbia, Afantou, Faliraki, Kallithea route and after 28 kms we are back in the city of Rhodes, having covered a total of 127 kms.

p. 128

The interior of the Byzantine, four-apse, Church of St Nicholas at Fountoukli, with fine wall-paintings of the fourteenth or fifteenth century.

p. 129 ➤

The four-apse Church of St Nicholas at Fountoukli.

2nd Route:

Cameiros - Embonas - Monolithos - Apolakia

On the second route we shall also be following the west coast of the island. Passing over green hills and valleys, we climb the grey rocky mountains, leaving behind the seashore with its deep-blue waters, to reach **Monolithos**, the lonely castle which stands on the edge of the sea looking out for pirates long forgotten.

Our first stopping-place on this route is ancient **Cameiros**, 32 kms from the city of Rhodes. Standing in the south-western part of the island, Cameiros was the smallest city of ancient Rhodes. The myth of Athlaemene, whom the citizens of Cameiros honoured and worshipped, indicates connections with Minoan Crete. Moreover, the discovery of Mycenaean cemeteries near the village of Kalavarda provides evidence of life in the area in Mycenean times. The city was orientated towards farming and stockbreeding and for that reason worshipped the so-called 'Mylantian' deities, whose name has to do with the mill and the grinding of grain.

The city flourished in Archaic times; its decline began in 408 BC with the unification of the Rhodians into the city of Rhodes. The settlement of ancient Cameiros stood in a hollow, of which the northern side went down to the sea and the southern ended in a kind of platform. The

p. 131 ➤

Aerial photograph of ancient Cameiros.

settlement itself developed on three levels. The first, the lowest, consisted of public buildings. The second, in the middle, extended in the shape of an amphitheatre over the slopes and was made up of houses, while the last was on the platform at the top and was occupied by the acropolis.

The Archaeological site of Ancient Cameiros

p. 132

View of ancient Cameiros, with the fountain and rectangular piazza in front.

A visit to the archaeological site of ancient Cameiros starts off from the 'piazza' with the public buildings. This is of an irregular shape, while the buildings on the site are divided into two complexes. One of these occupies the central, southern and western part and the other is at the north-eastern edge, on a raised level. In the middle of the south-western part can be seen the foundations of

a distyle Doric temple of the Hellenistic period (late third or early second century BC), which according to one view was dedicated to Pythian Apollo. Votive offerings began to be set up outside the eastern and northern side of the temple from the second half of the second century BC. There was a small Ionic temple at its north-eastern corner, in all probability itself a votive offering.

To the south-east of the Temple of Apollo, the remains of a fountain have survived. In front of this, to the north, there was an almost rectangular square. On its eastern side and on its north-eastern and south-eastern corner, directly opposite the Temple of Apollo, there were three steps, which must have served as seats for worshippers to watch the rites to the south and east of the temple, in the square. To the north of the square, a wall was later built, perhaps in the mid Hellenistic period, which closed it off on the north side. In front of this wall pedestals with votive offerings were set up.

To the north-east and outside the square with the fountain, there is a semi-circular platform, used by public speakers, and a sanctuary closed in on all four sides. Near this there are altars (eastern and western - the eastern being approximately one metre higher than the western), where sacrifices were made to the various deities. The western level is dominated by an oblong altar, which, as can be seen from an inscription on one of its sides, was dedicated to the sun-god. Two statues of *kouroi*, now to be seen in the Rhodes Archaeological Museum, were found in the area of the altars.

Outside the southern wall of the sacrifice area, a large staircase with 12 steps brings the visitor to the settlement's central road. Excavation has discovered public baths at the northern extermity of the road. The settlement's houses were to the east and west of the main road. Only a part of these has so far been excavated. In some of these houses which have survived in good condition, an inner courtyard - the atrium - surrounded by a colonnade can be seen. Further south, the road begins to climb and brings us to the highest point of the hill, the site of the acropolis of Cameiros at a height of 120 metres above sea level. This is where the Temple of Athena Polias stood. All that can be seen today are remains of the foundations of the temple and the precinct of the sanctuary.

The temple must have been peripteral, dating from the late third or early second century BC and in all probability replacing an earlier temple on the site which was destroyed by the earthquake of 226 BC. On the northern part of the hill there is a large cistern of the sixth or fifth century BC hewn out of the soft stone of the rock and capable of holding 600 cubic metres of water. Rainwater from the temple roof flowed into this and supplied the town by means of special channels.

In the late third or early second century BC, a large colonnade, of a length of approximately 200 metres, resting on two rows of Doric columns and orientated east-west, was built to the north of the Santuary of Athena. Behind the columns there were rooms which must have provided overnight accommodation for pilgrims attending religious ceremonies.

When the colonnade was built, the cistern went out of use. In its place, 16 deep wells, communicating with each other by means of underground channels, were sunk in the rooms of the colonnade.

After visiting ancient Cameiros, we return to the main road and, travelling west, arrive, after 14 kms, at **Skala Kamirou**. This is a little fishing village, from whose harbour caïques leave every day for the island of Chalki. To the south of Skala Kamirou, the castle of **Kastelo** perches on a wooded hill. This dates from the Byzantine period and was built to protect the western coast of Rhodes. It was rebuilt by the Knights of St John in the sixteenth century. Two side roads lead to the castle: one starts off

p. 135 ►

In most of the villages of Rhodes, particularly in mountain areas, the residents retain Greek customs in their completeness. In the photograph a village woman bakes bread rings in the traditional-style oven in the yard of her house.

some 500 metres after Skala Kamirou, while the starting-
point of the other is about 2 kms along the road. Visitors
should take the second, since the road is in better condition, though care is necessary in wet weather. Of the
castle, only the external fortification has survived, but the
view towards the bay at Glyfada and the islets of
Tragousa, Strongyli, Alymnia and Makri is magnificent.

We return to the main road, which continues south,
climbing between hills until it comes to **Kritinia**, a village which clings to the side of Mt Atavyros. Four kms

south of Kritinia there is a road junction. The road to the left leads, after 4 kms, to **Embonas**, the highest village on Rhodes at 850 metres. Here the residents still wear local costume and keep up their tradition of multi-coloured embroidery, while the houses provide a good idea of the traditional architectural style of Rhodes.

From Embonas it is possible, using the services of a guide, to climb to the summit of Atavyros (1,215 metres), where there was a sanctuary of Zeus. The climb is a fairly hard one and there is often a strong wind blowing at the summit. Those undertaking it should remember to take water with them and to be suitably dressed. From Embonas, the surfaced road continues, bringing us, after 14 kms, to the picturesque village of **Ayios Isidoros**.

On our return to the main road, we travel southwards. This route among the pine trees is one of the most attractive on the island. After 17 kms, we come to **Siana**, a village on the slopes of Akramitis, famous for its honey. Five kms south of Siana is the village of **Monolithos**. South-west of Monolithos, at a distance of 2 kms, the castle of the same name, built in the fifteenth century by the Knights, stands on the top of a lonely rock. A surfaced road leads to the foot of the rock; from this point, visitors to the castle must climb to the top on foot, but the fine view when they get there will amply reward them. Inside the castle there is a single-aisled church dedicated to St Pantaleimon.

p. 137 ➤

The Kritinia fortress crowns one of the peaks of Mt Atavyros. The imposing landscape with its sheer cliffs rising out of the sea rewards the efforts of walkers.

South of Monolithos, a path leads down to the sea, at **Fourni**. The picture which greets the visitor there is one composed of pines, golden beaches, sheltered coves and caves hollowed out of the soft rock.

After 10.5 kms, the road brings us to the village of **Apolakia**. From Apolakia an unsurfaced road leads to the deserted Byzantine monastery of Skiadi, some 11 kms further south. This is the farthest point on our second route, approximately 100 kms from the city of Rhodes.

3rd Route:

Kallithea - Faliraki - Lindos - Kattavia - Prassonisi

pp. 138-139

Two views of the hot springs of Kallithea. The building is the work of the Italians, but no longer functions.

Our third route completes our introduction to the island of Rhodes. This will take us to the east coast of the island with its charming villages and uncrowded beaches. Once again, our starting-point is the city of Rhodes, and our route will take us, 95 kms away, to Kattavia, the southernmost village on Rhodes, and from there to the extremity of the ´island at Prassonisi, to see a landscape which is all its own, against a background of a sea churned by the north-westerly winds.

We leave the city by Exit A. After 7 kms, we come to the village of **Koskinou** with its pretty houses, next to **Kallithea** (9 kms) with its medicinal springs, and then to **Faliraki** (12 kms). This former fishing village has developed into a major tourist resort with a large number of hotels strung out along its level sandy beach.

As the road leaves the seashore, it snakes among olive and fruit trees. **Afantou**, one of the largest villages on the island, is tucked in among the green hills. Its

p. 140

Two views of Faliraki. At a short distance from the city of Rhodes, what was once a small village has developed into one of the most cosmopolitan spots on the island. The night life continues until dawn throughout the summer.

name is said to be due to the fact that it was invisible ('áfanto') to pirates from the sea. Afantou is the centre for carpet-making for Rhodes. The village has a golf course, while only a kilometre from Afantou there is a long pebble beach with sparkling clear water. The Church of Our Lady 'Katholiki' on the way to the beach has wall-paintings of the seventeenth and eighteenth centuries. Four kms to the south is **Kolymvia**, which has most attractive sandy little coves some 2 kms from the village. After Kolymvia, a branch from the main road leads to the Byzantine monastery of **Tsambika**, dedicated to the Blessed Virgin. However, visitors should bear in mind that the road is in poor condition for about 2 kms, after which it turns into an uphill path. As we follow it, the view out to sea becomes increasingly impressive, while the beach at Tsambika is particularly beautiful, though it is approached by a rather difficult

p. 141

The whole of the east coast of Rhodes is scattered with tourist villages sloping down to busy beaches with organised facilities. The photograph shows the Kolymbia beach.

p. 143 ➤

*Two of the beaches
of Rhodes on its east
coast.*

p. 142

*The Tsambika beach
is one of the finest
on the island. Its
northern side is
closed in by a steep
hill, on the top of
which stands the
Byzantine
Monastery of
Tsambika,
dedicated to the
Blessed Virgin.*

downhill path, which begins about 300 metres after the turning to the monastery. It is worth persevering with this path, because it leads to one of the finest beaches on Rhodes. It can, however, also be reached by road. Our next stop is **Archangelos**, 6 kms after Kolymvia, a village with a pottery and carpet-making tradition. In the village itself, the Church of St John, with wall-paintings of the fourteenth century, can be visited. Nearby is the castle of the same name, built by Orsini, Grand Master of the Knights of St John. The climb to the castle takes 10 - 20 minutes.

To the south of the castle of Archangelos rises another fortification: **Faraklo**, one of the strongest fortresses on Rhodes, of the period of the Knights. It stands on a small headland between the bay of Malona and the bay of Vlycha. Here the climb to the top takes about 15 - 20 minutes.

After visiting Faraklo, we return to the main road and continuing in a southerly direction arrive at **Massari**. Four kms away is **Lindos**, one of the three city-states founded by the Dorians on the island.

A rocky hill rises between two sheltered bays. Its top is dominated by the acropolis of Lindos, a place charged with a history which goes back to the earliest human presence on the island. This rock, sheer towards the sea, has gentler slopes on its northern side. The white houses of the village with their pebble-paved court-yards and their narrow alleys start at the innermost point of the bay, which lies to the north of the acropolis, and mount to the foot of the rock. The acropolis is

p. 144

Lindos stands among imposing rocks which rise steeply from the sea, creating many idyllic little harbours.

reached on foot or on donkeys. The view from the top is unique: the bay of Lindos with its scores of fishing-boats on one side and on the other the calm waters of the cove of Ayios Pavlos, where tradition says that St Paul anchored in 57 AD.

According to mythology, it was Lindos, grandson of the sun-god Helios, who first colonised this place. Archaeological finds show that the area had been inhabited in the Neolithic age, while Mycenaean graves indicate the presence of Achaeans here too. The arrival of the Dorians in the twelfth and eleventh centuries BC, when they settled here, gave a boost to the development of Lindos. Standing at a point from which it could

p. 145

The attractive harbour of St Paul at Lindos. The chapel on the right was built to commemorate the visit of the Apostle Paul in 57 AD.

monitor the passage of vessels sailing in the eastern Aegean, Lindos, unlike Cameiros, developed a maritime character. From the eighth to the sixth century BC it was an important commercial centre for the region. In the seventh century it founded colonies at Gela and Acragas in Sicily and at Phasele on the shores of Pamphylia. In the sixth century, which was a period of great prosperity for Lindos, it was governed by Cleobulus, one of the Seven Sages of Greece.

Under his rule, its economy was boosted, major public works were undertaken, currency was minted on the Phoenician system (the trade of the Lindians was chiefly with Egypt and Phoenicia), the Temple of Lindian Athena was renovated, and the city was victorious in a war with Lycia. The decline of Lindos began in the fifth century BC.

With the setting up of the 'deme of the Rhodians', the city lost its importance, but without ever ceasing to be regarded as sacred or being abandoned, with the exception of the period between the sixth and the tenth century AD, when its inhabitants moved into the acropolis or to the hinterland.

The acropolis was the scene of important building works in the Hellenistic period. In Byzantine times and under the rule of the Knights, it was fortified, while in the latter period it became an administrative and judicial centre, with 12 Knights living there. It was here that in 1319, De Villaret, the first Grand Master of Knights of St John, took refuge to escape arrest by the Chapter of the Order.

The acropolis of Lindos was also used as a stronghold by the Turks. The last period of prosperity of the port and town of Lindos was in the fifteenth, sixteenth, and seventeenth centuries, from which its mansions date.

p. 149 ▶

The village of Lindos, at the foot of the acropolis, retains many features of an individualistic architecture, influenced by the island, Byzantine, medieval, and Arab styles.

The Archaeological site of Lindos

p. 151 ▶
The entrance to the Lindos acropolis.

p. 150

Part of the Doric colonnade of the Hellenistic period on the acropolis of Lindos, now restored.

The imposing rock which the first inhabitants of Lindos chose for their acropolis has a flat area at the top of a roughly triangular shape. This is the site of the ruins of the sanctuary of Athena.

The walls which surround the acropolis today are the fortifications built by the Knights of St John. The ancient walls were lower, allowing the buildings within to be visible from outside. Entry to the archaeological site is by way of the medieval walls and the steps built under the rule of the Knights and leading to the palace of the governor of the castle and from there to the main acropolis area.

On a platform before we come to the steps we can see on the left, on a rock, a carved semi-circular dais and the stern of a ship. On the broader part of the ship there is a base on which stood, according to the inscription, a statue of the admiral Agesander. This was a work of the second century BC, attributed to Pythocritus, the creator of the famous Victory of Samothrace.

Next to the medieval governor's quarters, within the area of the acropolis, are the remains of the Byzantine Church of St John, dating from the thirteenth century.

Further to the east, there is another semi-circular platform, on which stood the statue of Pamphilis and the bases of votive of-

ferings. At the north-eastern edge there are the remains of a small Roman temple. At the south-east of the platform, a staircase leads to a kind of raised square, supported on a row of arches (dating from the first century BC). From this square we enter the large Doric colonnade of the Hellenistic period. This colonnade, which has a Greek Π shape, is open to the north, in the opposite direction to the line of the Temple of Athena, and stands exactly in front of the Propylaeum. It is a work of 200 BC, with a length of 88 metres, a height of six, and a width of nine, and had a total of 42 columns, of which 20 are standing today. Behind the eight central columns of the colonnade, the steps leading to the Propylaeum begin. The Propylaeum, of which only the foundations remain, was built, like the steps, after 408 BC and was modelled on the Propylaea of the Parthenon in Athens.

It consisted of two rows of columns, one of which, on the north, formed a Π shape and had the same orienta-

p. 152

The theatre at Lindos, carved out of the rock on the western side of the acropolis. Today, 26 of its rows of seats remain.

tion as the Doric colonnade, while the other, on the south, was in the shape of an L, with two sides of unequal length, facing the temple. Between the rows of columns was a series of rooms, most of which were on the western side of the southern columns.

The Temple of Lindian Athena stands on the highest point of the acropolis. According to tradition, the first temple in the sanctuary was built around 1500 BC by Danaus, as an acknowledgement of the hospitality which he had received from the local inhabitants. In reality, the earliest temple of Athena was built in the Archaic period and was replaced in 330 BC by another, amphiprostyle (tetrastyle) Doric, temple.

The position of the temple and the layout of the buildings in the sanctuary of Lindos had, as a whole, something of a theatrical character, in keeping with the prevailing trend in the Hellenistic period. Thus, a series of colonnades and the Propylaeum hid the temple and suggested

p. 153

The sanctuary of Athena Lindia was built on a steep rock of a height of 115 metres, from which it was possible to monitor the sea round about. The Doric temple to the goddess was built on the highest point of the acropolis.

in worshippers a sense of a ritual ascent and of a gradual revelation of the divine, culminating on the extremity of the rock.

Before leaving the village of Lindos and its acropolis, the visitor should not omit to see the ancient theatre, which lies on the western side of the acropolis, carved out of the rock. Twenty-six of its *cunei* (rows of seats) survive. On the north side of the acropolis is the 'Bucopium', a small sanctuary of the tenth or ninth century BC where sacrifices of animals took place, while on the west is a Hellenistic tomb to which the name of the 'Tomb of Cleobulus' has been given. In the village itself there is the Church of Our Lady, in the shape of a cross with an octagonal dome. At its western door there is the device of the Grand Master D'Aubusson and an inscription with the dates 1489/90, probably because some addition was made to the building at that time. An inscription over the north door informs us that the wall-paintings in the church are the work of the artist Grigoris from Symi and are dated 1779.

Attention should also be drawn to the tradition of the Lindians in ceramics and particularly in the production of decorative plates. The practice of this art, which shows Eastern influences, goes back to the sixteenth century and was at its zenith in the sixteenth and seventeenth. Its themes are mostly taken from the plant world.

After our visit to Lindos, we return to the main road. We pass through village after village, most of them clinging to some hillside in the interior of the island. A road which sets out from **Lardos** and leads into the interior brings us to **Laerma**.

Four kms outside the village, at **Thari**, is the Church of the Archangel *(Taxiárchis)*, which has important wall-paintings of the twelfth and sixteenth centuries. The church, which was once the katholikon of a monastery, is at present closed. It can be visited by arrangements arrived at in the village of Laerma. The road by which it is reached is not surfaced. After Laerma, we come to **Asklipeios** (4 kms), where we can visit an eleventh-century Byzantine church and the ruins of a Venetian castle dating from around 1200. As we leave the interior of the island and see the calm sea on our left, we can leave the main road for a while and take a cooling swim. At **Plimmyri**, the last village on the eastern coast of Rhodes, there is a fine sandy beach. After that, the road again turns into the interior, bringing us, after 8 kms, to the island's southernmost village, **Kattavia**. Nine kms to the south of Kattavia, a path leads to **Prassonisi**.

Here there are dunes of clean sand and a narrow spit of sand links the land to the little headland with its lighthouse. In winter, this strip of sand is covered by the sea as it is whipped up by the wind, and the little headland becomes an island. On either side of the projection there is a cove, and, depending on the direction of the wind, when the waters of one of these are calm, those of the other are rough, and *vice versa*. And it is at this point that our exploration of this sun-drenched Aegean island comes to an end.

p. 157

Lindos.

Symi

The island, where according to tradition the Three Graces were born, has been inhabited since prehistoric times. The first settlers were the Lelegians. Later, sharing the history of the other Dodecanese, it witnessed a succession of conquerors (Argives, Rhodians, Romans, Byzantines). Under the rule of the Knights of St. John for about two centuries, it fell to the Turks in 1522. Thanks to its location along important trade routes, Symi began to develop economically. Symi was under Italian occupation from 1912 to 1945; it was here that the protocol ceding the Dodecanese to the Allies was signed at the end of the war.

The capital of the island has retained all its neo- classical elegance. Dominated by the castle of the Knights, it is divided into Ano (Upper) Symi (Hora) and the lower town (Yialo). Symi is noted for its long tradition in wood carving, and beautiful examples can still be seen in the island's houses. There are also a number of exquisite churches and monasteries containing fine carvings and mosaics, as , for example, the Megali Panayia of the Kastro , Megalos Sotiras, and others. Caiques are available to take one to the picturesque beaches (Nanou, Marathounta) and neighbouring islets. Generally speaking, Symi has undergone little tourist development as yet and is a fine place for those in search of peace and quiet.

p. 159 ➤

Symi.